RESEARCHING FAMILY HISTORY IN WALES

Compiled by

Jean Istance (Dyfed FHS)
and
E.E. Cann (Gwent FHS)

from information supplied by the
Family History Societies of Wales

Published by
The Federation of Family History Societies (Publications) Ltd.
The Benson Room,
Birmingham and Midland Institute,
Margaret Street, Birmingham B3 3BS
in association with the
Association of the Family History Societies of Wales

First published 1996

Copyright © Jean Istance and E.E. Cann

ISBN 1-86006-030-7

Printed and bound at The Alden Press, Oxford OX2 0EF

CONTENTS

INTRODUCTION

In 1993 the Association of Family History Societies of Wales published the book, *Welsh Family History: A Guide to Research* which has been read and appreciated by many who are researching the history of families in the original thirteen counties of Wales.

Even before the book was finished there were plans for a follow-up booklet which would give detailed information about the County Record Offices and Libraries of Wales which would be useful to researchers. The Association aims to provide, within this book, the location of archives and libraries, giving an outline of their resources with other general information including opening times, facilities for the disabled, incidental charges for entry or services and last, but not the least important, information on where to park.

It is presented in areas, beginning in the North East, then the North West, moving south through Central Wales to the counties of the South West then on across the south of the country, where Glamorgan is now seven new local authorities, to end in the South East. One or two new county names were adopted when the reorganisation of the local authorities came into force in April this year but the original county names are clearly identified in the index which follows.

We are grateful to all the Archivists, Librarians and members of the various branches of the Family History Societies who have co-operated in the production of this book. We hope that those of you with little knowledge of Wales but who are eager to trace your Welsh ancestry will want to visit the Principality and, while researching, enjoy the hospitality and scenery of Wales.

Wrth baratoi y llyfryn hwn 'roeddem yn meddwl am y rhai nad ydynt yn adnabod Cymru ond sy'n gwerthfawrogi eu llinach Cymraeg. Byddwn yn hapus iawn i feddwl efallai bydd y Cymry Cymraeg, sy'n adnabod ein gwlad yn dda, yn medru darganfod rhywbeth o ddiddordeb yma hefyd.

NORTH EAST WALES

DENBIGHSHIRE

Denbighshire was created in 1536 under the Act of Union in the reign of Henry VIII. It was formed from the lordships of Denbighland (cantrefs of Rhos and Rhufoniog), Ruthin (cantref of Dyffryn Clwyd), Bromfield and Ial (cantref of Maelor Gymraeg), Chirk (cantref of Swydd y Waun), Moldsdale (commote of Ystrad Alun), and the commote of Rhuddlan. In 1541, Moldsdale and Rhuddlan were transferred to the county of Flint. In 1974 Denbighshire was combined with Flintshire to form the county of Clwyd which was abolished in 1996 when four new unitary authorities, Conwy, Denbighshire, Flintshire and Wrexham, were created. Although the new Denbighshire and Flintshire have the same names as the historic counties which existed before 1974, their boundaries are different. As a rule of thumb, local historical records will be found in the appropriate record office which was in existence prior to 1974.

The area of Wales which became the old county of Denbigh had a turbulent past. Part was in Gwynedd and part in Powys and as a border area would have seen its share of fighting, with the land in the east liable to incursions from the Anglo-Saxon kingdom of Mercia. In 1066, William of Normandy invaded England and by 1070 had subdued Mercia. The two centuries which followed saw the establishment of the marcher lordships in the areas under the Normans and in 1282 Edward I, king of England, conquered Wales but that tended to make this area more peaceful.

The old county of Denbigh occupied a central position in the north of Wales. Its northern extent was the twelve miles of coastline on the Irish Sea and it extended south from the sea to the mountainous border with Merioneth, where the mountains reach 2,300 feet in height. In the east, it stretched from the Clwydian range of hills that formed the Flintshire border and the River Dee that bordered Cheshire and

Shropshire, west to the Conwy valley beyond which was Snowdonia in the county of Caernarfon. The valleys of the Dee, Clwyd, Conwy and Ceiriog contrast with the moors and mountains of Hiraethog. Set amid this beautiful scenery are many charming villages with some of the oldest churches in Wales and towns which are diverse in character. Wrexham, in the east, is an industrial town and the largest in the north of Wales. Llangollen, in the south, is well known for its annual International Eisteddfod. Llanrwst stands on the River Conwy on the western edge of the county and in the centre are the historic boroughs of Ruthin and Denbigh, both of which have castles. On the coast are the popular seaside resorts of Colwyn Bay and Abergele which offer the tourist many attractions. The population of the county in the 1971 census was 184,824 people, most of whom were concentrated around Colwyn Bay and Wrexham. The remainder of the county was rural and comparatively sparsely populated.

The area that was Denbighshire is an important agricultural area. There is arable farming in the valleys and a market garden area at Holt on the banks of the River Dee as well as cattle raising, sheep farming and dairy production. The main markets for the county are at Denbigh, Ruthin and Wrexham, although smaller markets are held at other towns. There has been a programme of reforestation and the Forestry Commission has the third largest forest in Wales, at Clocaenog.

Industry is mainly confined to the eastern part of the county. Traditional industries are the manufacture of iron, steel, textiles and bricks, brewing, coal and lead mining, with the quarrying of slate and limestone.

DENBIGHSHIRE RECORD OFFICE

46 Clwyd Street, Ruthin, Denbighshire LL15 1HP
Tel: (01824) 703077
Fax: (01824) 705180

Opening hours
Monday–Thursday   9.00 a.m.–4.45 p.m.
Friday   9.00 a.m.–4.15 p.m.

A County Archives Research Network (CARN) *Reader's Ticket* is required which is available from the office on production of suitable identification (see p. 67 for details). An *appointment* is necessary for the use of the film and fiche readers.

Holdings

Denbighshire County Council records (1889–1974)

Denbighshire Quarter Sessions records from 1649

Denbighshire and Flintshire census returns 1841–1891 (microfilm copies)

Census indexes for all Welsh counties in the 1881 census (microfiche)

Denbighshire and Flintshire Parish Registers (microfilm)

St. Asaph diocese Bishop's Transcripts (incomplete) (microfilm)

Calendars of Probate, England and Wales 1858–1928

Wills, abstracts and indexes for the dioceses of
  St. Asaph 1557–1832 (microfiche)
  Bangor 1635–1833 (microfiche)
  Llandaff 1746–1832 (microfiche)
  St. David 1564–1837 (microfiche)

Tithe maps and apportionments

Non-parochial registers prior to 1838 (microfilm); index available

Denbighshire Poor Law and school records

Denbighshire Hearth Tax returns 1663–1671 (microfilm)

Denbighshire Electoral Registers

St. Catherine's House indexes to births, marriages and deaths 1837–1865

Collections of deeds, estate and family papers

International Genealogical Index (I.G.I.) for Wales (microfiche)

A personal name index computer printout is available; this is an on-going project.

LIBRARIES

Ruthin Library
Record Street, Ruthin, Denbighshire LL15 1DS
Tel: (01824) 705274
Fax: (01824) 705274

Local history collection

REGISTRATION OF BIRTHS, DEATHS AND MARRIAGES

Denbighshire South District
The Register Office
Station Road, Ruthin, Denbighshire LL15 1BS
Tel: (01824) 703782

Denbighshire North District
    The Register Office
    Morfa Hall, Church Street, Rhyl, Denbighshire LL18 3AA
    Tel: (01745) 353428

WELSH TOURIST INFORMATION NETWORK

Most centres are open between 10 a.m. and 5.30 p.m.
    Colwyn Bay Tel: (01492) 530478
    Llangollen   Tel: (01978) 860828
    Ruthin   Tel: (01824) 703992
    Wrexham   Tel: (01978) 292015

CLWYD FAMILY HISTORY SOCIETY RESOURCE CENTRE

This is at the Baptist Cemetery, Mwrog Street, Ruthin. The centre is manned by volunteers and is open most Saturdays, but you should always contact the Society first just in case it is not open. The centre is open to members only, but you may join on the spot. It contains useful information and references among which are
I.G.I. 1992 edition for the whole country
1891 census for Clwyd
1881 census and indexes for England and Wales (microfiche)
1851 census indexes from neighbouring Family History Societies
1851 census indexes for several local areas
Index and transcripts of Denbighshire and Flintshire Nonconformist
    registers pre 1838
Index to wills in Denbighshire R.O.
Family Registry (Genealogical Society of Utah), 1989 edition
    (microfiche)
Catalogue of Welsh material at Salt Lake City, 1988 edition
    (microfiche)
Welsh Genealogies AD300–1400 by Bartrum 1974 (microfiche)
The Liverpool Volunteers 1759–1803 (microfiche)
Copies of all published Parish Registers for Flintshire and
    Denbighshire. (Order forms for these are available from the centre
    or the Society.)

DISABLED FACILITIES

All the above places can cope with access for the disabled, though in some cases with difficulty. Other facilities such as suitable toilets may be lacking and the Clwyd FHS resource centre has no toilets at all; the nearest public toilets are quite a walk away.

FLINTSHIRE

Flintshire was one of the six Welsh counties created by Edward I subsequent to the conquest of Wales in 1284. It consisted at that time of the commotes of Prestatyn and Coleshill in the cantref of Tegeingl (or Englefield), Hopedale and Maelor Saesneg, three detached areas. In 1541, the lordship of Moldsdale (the commote of Ystrad Alun) and the townships of Marford and Hoseley, with the commote of Rhuddlan, were transferred from Denbighshire to Flintshire, linking most of the county together with the exception of Maelor Saesneg which remained detached. Flintshire was combined with Denbighshire in 1974 and became the new county of Clwyd, which was abolished in 1996.

The northern part of the vale of Clwyd and the coastal area includes the cathedral city of St. Asaph with its memorial commemorating the translation of the Bible into Welsh in 1588. The town of Rhuddlan has an imposing Edwardian castle and the seaside resorts of Rhyl and Prestatyn are popular holiday centres. Dairy farming is the main occupation of the farms, which are quite large by Welsh standards.

The Dee estuary forms the northern boundary of Flintshire. This area includes the town of Holywell, famous for St. Winifred's Well, one of the Seven Wonders of Wales. At Greenfield, near Holywell, are the ruins of the 12th century Cistercian Abbey of Basingwerk. Flint Castle was the first castle built by Edward I during his conquest of Wales and Flint town was granted a charter by him in 1284. This area of Deeside has long been an industrial area, with coal mines at Bagillt, lead mines near Halkyn, steel works at Shotton, chemical and artificial silk works at Flint and brick works at Buckley. Mostyn Quay was of great importance for the export of coal to Ireland.

The rural upland area of the county includes the towns of Mold and Caerwys. Mold, the home town of the 19th century Welsh novelist Daniel Owen, has a 15th century parish church which is one of the finest in Wales. At Caerwys, in 1568, the first Welsh Eisteddfod since the 13th century was held. Following the granting of a charter to the town of Caerwys by Edward I in 1290, a rectangular street plan was laid out.

Maelor Saesneg, or 'Flintshire Detached' as it became known, lies to the east of Denbighshire. This is a prosperous agricultural area and includes the town of Bangor Iscoed, or Bangor-on-Dee, the site of a great 6th century Celtic monastery. The nearby town of Overton has a 15th century church with famous yew trees in its churchyard, another of the Seven Wonders of Wales.

FLINTSHIRE RECORD OFFICE

The Old Rectory, Hawarden, Deeside, Flintshire CH5 3NR
Tel: (01244) 532364
Fax: (01244) 538344

Opening hours

Monday–Thursday   9.00 a.m.–4.45 p.m.
Friday   9.00 a.m.–4.15 p.m.

A CARN *Reader's Ticket* is required. This is available from the office on production of suitable identification. An *appointment* is required for the use of the microfiche and film readers.

Holdings

Official archives include those of

Flintshire County Council (from 1889 to 1974)
Quarter Sessions for Flintshire from 1720
Census indexes for all Welsh counties for 1881 (microfiche)
St. Asaph diocese Bishop's Transcripts (incomplete) (microfilm)
St. Asaph diocese register of copy wills, 1565–1709 (microfilm)
Flintshire electoral registers
Deeside Shipping, crew lists and agreements, index available
First World War records; card index giving details of over 10,600
    Flintshire men who served in the armed forces
Wills, abstracts and indexes for the dioceses of
    St. Asaph 1557–1832 (microfiche)
    Bangor 1635–1833 (microfiche)
    Llandaff 1746–1832 (microfiche)
    St. David 1564–1837 (microfiche)
All Flintshire Parish Registers. Transcribed and indexed copies of most registers are available for inspection at Hawarden and Ruthin. (These can also be obtained from Clwyd FHS; for further information see under Denbighshire.)

A series of leaflets explaining the resources of the office has been prepared (list available).

LIBRARIES

Reference and Information Centre
Library Headquarters
County Civic Centre, Mold, Flintshire CH7 6NW
Tel: (01352) 702495

Opening hours
Monday–Thursday   8.45 a.m.–5.00 p.m.
Friday   8.45 a.m.–4.30 p.m.

Holdings
One of the best county collections of books on local history in Wales
local newspapers (microfilm)
the complete St. Catherine's House indexes 1837–1940 (microform)
An *appointment* is necessary to use the readers.

Rhyl
Museum and Arts Centre, Church Street, Rhyl, Flintshire LL18 3AA
Tel: (01745) 353814
Fax: (01745) 331438

Local and Welsh history collection
1881 census for Rhyl area and local newspapers on microfilm

Connah's Quay
Wepre Drive, Connah's Quay, Deeside, Flintshire CH5 4HA
Tel: (01244) 830485

Local collection with photographs
Some Deeside shipping

FACILITIES

All the above buildings can offer access for the disabled (though some with difficulty). Other facilities, such as suitable toilets, may be lacking.

REGISTRATION OF BIRTHS, DEATHS AND MARRIAGES

Alyn and Deeside District
The Register Office, Old Rectory, Hawarden, Deeside, Flintshire
Tel: (01244) 531512

Delyn District
The Register Office
Park Lane, Holywell, Flintshire CH8 7UR
Tel: (01352) 711813

Rhuddlan District
The Register Office
Morfa Hall, Church Street, Rhyl, Flintshire LL18 3AA
Tel: (01745) 353428

WELSH TOURIST INFORMATION NETWORK

Local centres mostly open between 10 a.m. and 5.30 p.m.

Ewloe   Tel: (01244) 541597
Mold   Tel: (01352) 759331
Rhyl   Tel: (01745) 355068
Prestatyn Tel: (01745) 854365 (summer only)

CHURCH OF JESUS CHRIST OF LATTER-DAY SAINTS FAMILY HISTORY CENTRE

171 Vale Road, Rhyl, Flintshire
Tel: (01745) 331172

The centre has a growing collection of microfilm and microfiche records relating to the local area. Copies of film and fiche records held in the Genealogical Society of Utah Library in Salt Lake City, USA may be ordered, for a small fee to cover costs, for viewing in the centre.

CONWY COUNTY BOROUGH COUNCIL

On April 1st 1996, Conwy County Borough Council was formed. We are informed that

"The services provided at Llandudno and Colwyn Bay Libraries will remain as at present although it is intended that the Headquarters function of the Library, Information and Archive Service will be based at the Llandudno building before the Autumn.

Archive records will remain in their previous office at either Caernarfon or Ruthin until such time as an Archive Service is established in this Authority. The Archive Access Point will remain at Llandudno Library."

LIBRARIES

Conwy Archive Service, Llandudno Library
Mostyn Street, Llandudno, Conwy LL30 2RP
Tel: (01492) 860101

This is a local authority archive service point consisting of microfilms of documents of local interest. Further provision for archives will be made in due course.

Opening hours

Monday and Thursday	10.00 a.m.–7.00 p.m.
Tuesday and Friday	10.00 a.m.–5.30 p.m.
Wednesday	10.00 a.m.–5.00 p.m.
Saturday	10.00 a.m.–1.00 p.m.

There is no *Car parking* available at the library.

Disabled facilities are available.

Holdings
Census returns and index to census returns
Local newspapers dating from 1895 (microfiche)
Trade Directories
I.G.I.
Current electoral roll (past rolls are sent on to the Caernarfon archives)
Memorial Inscriptions for the area

Three film and fiche readers are available.

Colwyn Bay Library
Woodlands Road West, Colwyn Bay, Conwy LL29 7DH
Tel: (01492) 532358

Holdings
Records available include
Local history collection
A collection of bound, year by year, local newspapers

An *appointment* is necessary for the use of readers.

Disabled facilities: a ramp and lift are available.

REGISTRATION OF BIRTHS, DEATHS AND MARRIAGES
Colwyn District
The Register Office
67 Market Street, Abergele LL22 7AG
Tel: (01745) 823976

TOURIST OFFICE
1 Chapel Street, Llandudno LL30 2SY
Tel: (01492) 876413)

PLACES OF INTEREST
Great Orme Coppermine Museum
Chardon Trust Museum (Private)
17 Gloddaeth Avenue, Llandudno

WREXHAM COUNTY BOROUGH COUNCIL

WREXHAM ARCHIVE SERVICE
County Buildings, Regent Street, Wrexham LL11 1RB
Tel: (01978) 358916

A local authority archive service point consisting of microfilms of documents of local interest. Further provision for archives will be made in due course.

WREXHAM LIBRARY AND ARTS CENTRE
Rhosddu Road, Wrexham LL11 1AU
Tel: (01978) 261932
Fax: (01978) 361876
Opening hours
Monday–Friday   9.00 a.m.–7.00 p.m.
Saturday   9.00 a.m.–12.30 p.m.
Holdings
Reference library for local and Welsh history
local newspapers from the 1850s (original and microfilm)
Census returns: 1891 for the whole area
other census years for the Wrexham area
local deed collection
An *appointment* is necessary for the use of readers.

REGISTRATION OF BIRTHS, DEATHS AND MARRIAGES
The Register Office,
2 Grosvenor Road, Wrexham LL11 1DL
Tel: (01978) 265786

NORTH WEST WALES

ISLE OF ANGLESEY/YNYS MON

A knowledge of local history can provide the student of family history with valuable background information and this is particularly true of Anglesey, bearing in mind the island's position as an important sea-route from the earliest times. The wandering saints of the Celtic church made use of such sea-routes and there are in Anglesey seventy parish churches traditionally associated with these saints. The influence of the Norsemen also survives in place names, including 'Anglesey' itself derived from the personal name 'Ongull'.

In the Middle Ages, Edward I made Anglesey a county and established a borough and castle at Beaumaris. The borough was originally intended as an English colony around the new castle and many of the burgesses, including the prestigious Bulkeley family, came from Cheshire and the border counties. Gradually, however, Welsh families were admitted and the borough flourished as a trading centre. An interesting indication of the kind of personal names used in Anglesey during the Medieval period may be seen in the Anglesey Submissions of 1406, for example William ap Madog ap Goronwy and Ieuan ap Dafydd ap Bleddyn. This is a list of over two thousand men who were forced to submit to the King, and fined, after the failure of the Owain Glyn Dwr rebellion.

The influence of the early Industrial Revolution was felt in Anglesey during the second half of the eighteenth century. Parys Mountain, near Amlwch, became the centre of the British copper industry and workers from many parts of the country, including Derbyshire, Cornwall and Swansea, found employment there as miners and smelters. Workers and their families also migrated there from other parts of Anglesey and Caernarfonshire. Amlwch grew rapidly from being a small coastal hamlet to having a population of nearly 5,000 in 1801. The names of those employed at the copper mines may be seen in the Mona Mine MSS at the University College of North Wales archives.

The construction of the new post road and railway across Anglesey during the first half of the nineteenth century resulted in many migrant workers moving into the area. Major improvements were also carried out at the port of Holyhead and the population of the town increased from under 4,000 in 1841 to nearly 9,000 ten years later. Later in the century, however, there was considerable rural depopulation and many workers and their families left the island to find work on Merseyside and in other areas.

ANGLESEY COUNTY RECORD OFFICE/ARCHIFDY YNYS MON

Department of Leisure and Heritage,
Shirehall, Llangefni, Anglesey/Ynys Môn LL77 7TW
Tel: (01248) 752562 (Ext. 271 or 269)

Opening hours
Monday–Friday   9.00 a.m.–1.00 p.m. and 2.00 p.m.–5.00 p.m.
Closed for Public Holidays and the first full week in November.
An appointment required for the use of film and fiche readers.

Car parking
Limited

Disabled facilities
Arrangements can be made to study documents at ground floor level provided advance notice is given.

Reader's ticket
A CARN ticket is required.

Holdings
All census returns from 1841 to 1891 for Anglesey.
Original public records, and some on microfilm: local authority, family, business, photographs, old county of Anglesey.

Postal Research
Detailed researches by prior payment.
Charges: first half hour £8.81 including V.A.T., then £2.94 per quarter hour including V.A.T.

Address for postal enquiries
Anglesey County Record Office,
Department of Leisure and Heritage,
Isle of Anglesey County Council,
Swyddfa'r Sir, Llangefni, Anglesey/Ynys Môn LL77 7TW

Facilities
Toilets on the premises.
No facilities for refreshments but cafes and public houses are only five
minutes away.

Publications
A list of holdings is available for inspection.

Llangefni Library
Department of Leisure and Heritage
Lôn y Felin, Llangefni, Anglesey/Ynys Môn LL77 7RT
Tel: (01248) 752092 (Information and Local Studies Section)

REGISTRATION OF BIRTHS, DEATHS AND MARRIAGES
The Superintendent Registrar
Isle of Anglesey County Council/Cyngor Sir Ynys Môn
Swyddfa'r Sir, Llangefni, Ynys Môn/Anglesey LL77 7TW
Tel: (01248) 752564

TOURIST OFFICE
Station site, Llanfairpwll LL61 5UJ
Tel: (01248) 713177

PLACES OF INTEREST
Oriel Ynys Môn, Llangefni
Museum of Childhood, Beaumaris
Beaumaris Gaol
Plas Newydd, Llanfairpwll
Menai Suspension Bridge

CAERNARFONSHIRE

The former counties of CAERNARFON and MERIONETH became
GWYNEDD COUNCIL on APRIL 1st 1996.

Following the reorganisation of Local Government in 1974,
Caernarfonshire became part of the larger county of Gwynedd, which
comprised the original counties of Anglesey, Caernarfonshire and
Merionethshire. The now-pending reorganisation will break up the
county again and the original county of Caernarfon will disappear once
more.

Throughout its history the chief industries have been farming and
slate quarrying, Dinorwic and Bethesda Quarries being the two largest

slate quarries in the world, each employing about 3,000 men. In their heyday, they exported their slates to all parts of the world from the ports of Caernarfon, Y Felinheli and Port Penrhyn, Bangor. Dinorwic Quarry has been closed for years and Bethesda Quarry is working on a much lesser scale than in the past. For the family historian it is fortunate that the records of Dinorwic Quarry have been deposited in the County Record Office in Caernarfon. This Record Office holds all the available Parish Registers for the county and in addition a considerable number of local newspapers.

The family historian is very fortunate to have access to the Archives Department of the University College of North Wales at Bangor and included in their collection is the 'Porth yr Aur Papers' of Caernarfon. This may be one of the most important collections of private papers in North Wales, being the accumulated papers of several solicitors in Caernarfon who had acted for a large number of small estates in the county. This collection has been extensively catalogued and will prove invaluable to researchers. It cannot be over-emphasised that knowledge of local history is very important and throws light on the movement of population from one area to another.

Caernarfonshire, like a number of other Welsh counties, has experienced periods of extreme depression which has meant large numbers of people emigrating to the United States of America. To assist researchers, the Gwynedd Family History Society has produced, *A selected list of Emigrants from Gwynedd to the USA, 1795–1932*, available on microfiche only, which is well worth looking at to find that elusive ancestor.

The hinterland of the Peninsula consists entirely of rural parishes with Porthmadog and Pwllheli being the biggest towns. With the county's considerable coastline it is not surprising that boat building has played an important part in the past, particularly at Caernarfon, the county town, Nefyn, Pwllheli and Portmadog.

Apart from the usual Church records it is important to remember that the county is predominantly Nonconformist and it is advisable to look at the records of the various chapels.

Today, the holiday industry plays an important part in the economy of the county, but it is not a new development. The wild and rugged mountains of Snowdonia have attracted visitors from time immemorial. It has been a favourite visiting place of tourists in the past from the days of Geraldus Cambrensis in 1188, when he made his famous tour of Wales, and many eminent tourists have followed in his footsteps.

GWYNEDD ARCHIVES AND MUSEUMS

County Offices,
Caernarfon, Gwynedd LL54 7EF
Tel: (01286) 679095

Opening hours
Monday–Friday   9.30 a.m.–12.30pm and 1.30 p.m.–5.00 p.m.
Wednesday   1.30 p.m.–7.00 p.m.

Car parking
Limited, but there is a public car park nearby.

Disabled facilities: Available

Reader's Ticket: CARN

Holdings
Parish records
Census returns
Estate records
Quarry records, etc.

Appointments
An appointment is required for microfilm and microfiche readers
  only.

Postal research
Charges: first half hour £8.81 including V.A,T., then £2.94 per quarter
hour including V.A.T..

Facilities
There are no facilities for refreshments.

UNIVERSITY OF WALES, BANGOR
Department of Manuscripts

The Library
University of Wales, Bangor, Gwynedd LL57 2DG
Tel: (01248) 351151 Ext. 2966
Enquiries to Archivist and Keeper of Manuscripts.

Opening hours
In term: Monday, Tuesday, Thursday, Friday: 9.00 a.m.–4.45 p.m.
              Wednesday: 9.00 a.m.–8.50 p.m.
In vacation: Monday–Friday   9.30 a.m.–4.45 p.m.
Generally open to the public; prior arrangement preferred.

The library of the University of Wales has been an approved
repository since 1927 and is a recognised place of deposit for public
records.

Car parking
There are no car parking facilities.

Holdings
Holdings run to some 500,000 items including Family and Estate, Mine and Quarry papers. Quarter Sessions records for the Borough of Beaumaris. Records of the University, including student registers 1884 - 1944.

Library facilities
Catalogues and indexes (Bangor MSS cataloguing is continually in progress).
Provisional guide to special collections (typescript)
Photocopying
Photography
Micro film/fiche readers.

REGISTRATION OF BIRTHS, DEATHS AND MARRIAGES
Institute Buildings
Pavilion Hill, Caernarfon, Gwynedd

TOURIST OFFICE
Castle Street, Caernarfon
Tel: (01268) 672232

PLACES OF INTEREST
Caernarfon Castle is in the immediate vicinity.
Royal Welch Fusiliers Regimental Museum,
The Castle, Caernarfon, Gwynedd LL55 2AY
Tel: (01286) 673362.

MERIONETHSHIRE/MEIRIONNYDD

The former counties of CAERNARFON and MERIONETH became GWYNEDD COUNCIL on APRIL 1st 1996.

Meirionnydd, the district council area 1974–1996, formed the greater part of the old Merionethshire, together with the cwmwd (commote) of Edeyrnion, the area between Corwen and Bala. Merionethshire was formed in 1284 but did not reach its later administrative definition until 1536. It has always been an agricultural area, with some good land in the fertile valleys and coastal strip, but much poorer land on higher ground and mountains, bearing livestock rather than crops in general. For many centuries agriculture was almost the only livelihood, together with associated industries, notably those related to the woollen industry (especially in the Dolgellau, Dinas Mawddwy and Bala areas) and mills and leatherworking. The area, therefore, consisted of small market towns and villages; small scale mineral extraction made little impact before the 19th century. The other main source of income was the sea with shipbuilding and trading with small vessels from such ports as Aberdyfi, Penmaenpool and Barmouth.

From a population of 9,000 in 1300, the 19th century brought a dramatic increase in population from 29,506 in 1801 to 52,038 in 1881. This was due mainly to the development of the slate industry, most notably in the Ffestiniog area (which saw an increase in population from 1,648 to 11,274 between 1831 and 1881) but also in the Corris, Abergynolwyn and Glyndyfrdwy areas. The drainage of marshy areas around rivers such as the Glaslyn, with the management of the larger estates and the building of the railways, all caused an increase in population but by the early 20th century the county was declining economically. The slate industry had slumped and there was migration, not only to the coalfields of South Wales and the North East and Midlands of England but overseas, especially to the United States of America. Partly due to the use of machinery, fewer workers were needed on the land and together with the decline of some great estates this caused rural depopulation. However, the 20th century saw the development of the coastal strip into a tourist and retirement area with increased military usage and the development of water and nuclear power causing great movement of population.

The county itself is widely different in its links. In some ways it is the stereotype of rural isolation but in fact workers in the agricultural sector travelled quite widely along routes unfamiliar to the traffic of today, following old drovers' roads and trackways over the mountains. In the east of the county, the link was strong with parts of Denbighshire (also being part of the diocese of St. Asaph). In the south, although the River Dyfi is a barrier in today's eyes, the link with Maldwyn (Montgomeryshire) was strong. To the north, workers in agriculture and the slate industry reflected the relationship with Caernarfonshire, especially with Eifionydd and Penmachno and later with Anglesey. Those involved in the maritime sector, as sailors and investors, had strong connections with other seaboard towns in North and West Wales and beyond.

Since Merionethshire was a county of small and larger estates (sometimes linked by marriage with estates elsewhere) the records at the Archives Offices at Dolgellau and Caernarfon, at the National Library of Wales and at the Archives of the University of North Wales at Bangor can prove to be very useful. However, since the county had many very small holdings, many of the records have not survived, but the maps and schedules of the Tithe apportionment are a valuable source of land information.

For background, *Atlas Meirionnydd* (Gwasg y Sir, 1974) (in Welsh only) is very useful in its narrative and maps. *The History of Merioneth* (Volume 1, Merioneth Historical and Record Society, 1967) is of less value to family historians, having only reached the 13th century; Volume 2 has been in the planning stage for years. The Society also publishes a useful annual journal. However, a number of histories of local areas such as *Cantref Meirionnydd* by R.P.Morris (Dolgellau, 1890) for the south of the county exist, many of which are only available in Welsh. There is a growing body of literature about the maritime and industrial history of Meirionnydd. From the later 19th and early 20th centuries there is a substantial body of histories, again in Welsh, on the various Nonconformist denominations and churches, which are a rich and greatly undervalued source of family history.

Indexes to the sources of history in Merioneth are poor, with two notable exceptions, i.e. those compiled and published by the Gwynedd Family History Society to marriages, graveyards and census records and the *Calendar of the Merioneth Quarter Session Rolls, Vol.1: 1733–65* (Merioneth County Council, 1965). The card indexes at both the Archives Office and the Library at Dolgellau form a welcome addition to published sources and are of value to family historians. The census for the county on microfilm is held at the County Archives.

MERIONETH RECORD OFFICE

Cae Penarlag, Dolgellau LL40 2YB
Tel: (01341) 422341 Ext. 3300 or 3301

Opening hours
Monday–Friday   9.00 a.m.–1.00 p.m. and 2.00 p.m.–5.00 p.m.
Closed annually during the first full week in November.

Car parking
Ample car parking is available.

Disabled facilities
There is a ramp approach to a single-storey building, no steps.
Wide doors to Research/Reading Room and toilets.

Appointment system

Appointments are advised for film and fiche readers.

Document ordering

It is not necessary to order documents in advance.

Holdings

Local Government Authority records and deposited local collections.
Bangor and St. Asaph Diocese Parish Records
Census, Merioneth only; County of Gwynedd 1891.

Postal research

Charges: first half hour £8.81 including V.A.T., then £2.94 per quarter hour including V.A.T.

Facilities

No refreshment facilities available.

Publications

Gwynedd Library and Archive Services Publications.
Calendar of Merioneth Quarter Sessions, K. William Jones.

REGISTRATION OF BIRTHS, DEATHS AND MARRIAGES

Register Office
South Meirionnydd
Bridge Street, Dolgellau LL40 1AU

Register Office
Ardudwy
Bryn Marian
Church Street
Blaenau Ffestiniog LL41 3HD

TOURIST OFFICE

Ty Meirion
Eldon Square
Dolgellau, Gwynedd
Tel: (01341) 422888

PLACES OF INTEREST

Ty Meirion (Quakers' Exhibition)
Plas Nannau, Llanfrachreth
Gwynfynydd Gold Mine
Cymmer Abbey

CENTRAL WALES

POWYS

Powys, one of the three ancient kingdoms of Wales, originally covered northern Montgomeryshire and parts of Denbighshire and Shropshire. It eventually extended its borders to include all of Montgomeryshire and Radnorshire and its influence stretched south over ancient Brycheiniog. It is these three counties, created by the Act of Union in 1536, which were brought together in 1974 to create a new authority with a familiar and ancient name. Powys County Council's County Archives Office serves as the authorised repository for the public and official records of both the new county of Powys and the three old counties. Created as recently as 1991, it has expanded its collections to include the records of the Quarter Sessions, estate records, Nonconformist records and collections of private correspondence.

The Archives Office also provides a co-ordinating and support service to the local studies sections of the Powys County Library, the sister services working together to provide better facilities for researchers. The County Archives Office has acquired microfilm copies of the Parish Registers for the whole of Powys, and copies of the Tithe maps and schedules from the National Library of Wales. A Local Studies Handbook has also been produced for library staff throughout the county which will help them assist researchers with their projects.

BRECONSHIRE

The county of Breconshire (or Brecknock) existed from 1536 to 1974, when it became the southern end of the new County of Powys. Geographically, it is divided by a range of mountains running east–west (the Brecknock Beacons and their continuation, the Black Mountains), which consist of Devonian rocks rising to nearly 1000 metres. Two major rivers, the Usk (in Welsh, Wysg) and the Wye (Gwy) drain from the north-west to the south and east. Both are major salmon rivers. Their valleys provide the only practical access to the County and have been heavily defended and contested throughout history. First came the Romans in about AD 60, then the Anglo-Saxons during the Dark Ages, and finally the Normans around 1080. Each wave has left evidence of its occupation, and this is especially well demonstrated at Tretower, where a Norman Castle and a mediaeval fortified Manor House are both open to the public.

The principal towns are Brecon (Aberhonddu) in the centre, Crickhowell (Crughywel) in the south, Hay (Y Gelli) in the east and Builth Wells (Llanfair ym Muallt) in the north, though all of these are only small market towns. In the south-west, the River Tawe runs through Coal Measure rocks towards Swansea and this area (around Ystradgynlais) has been subjected to industrialisation. Elsewhere, the county remains unspoilt and the chief occupation continues to be sheep rearing and forestry. Our Breconshire ancestors, were they to return today, would recognise most of the county as scarcely altered since their day.

The main attraction for visitors is the scenery. There are several hundred square miles of unfenced mountain for walkers and climbers to roam at will, while in the south-west, near Ystradfellte, there are caves and spectacular limestone gorges where the rivers Hepste and Mellte pour over a succession of waterfalls.

However, this is not all. Hay contains the world's largest collections of second hand books. Librarians from many countries come here to replenish their stocks, while many book lovers come to browse and find a bargain. In May there is a literary festival in this town, providing a platform for many of the major British literary figures. On a lighter note, Brecon hosts a jazz festival each August. But for those with Breconshire ancestors who want to see something of the agricultural way of life, undoubtedly the best opportunity would be the Royal Welsh Show at Builth Wells, held in the third week of July.

MONTGOMERYSHIRE

It does not take long to realise that the valleys and uplands of Montgomeryshire contain some of the loveliest scenery in the British Isles. Known to the early bards as 'Powys paradwys Cymru' (Powys, the paradise of Wales), the ancient Kingdom of Powys split into the two princedoms of north and south in 1160.

The rulers of the southern portion skilfully trod the political and military tight-rope of self-preservation, siding now with their overlord Welsh Princes of Wales and now with the English kings until their inheritance passed by marriage to the Norman family of the Charltons in 1309. Thereafter the area existed as an English barony until the Act of Union in 1536 formed it into the county of Montgomery. It stayed as such until the Local Government Act of 1972 regrouped it with the shires of Radnor and Brecon to the south to create in 1974 the new and much larger modern county of Powys.

This decline from a 10th century kingdom to a 20th century district has not, however, affected the independence of thought of its inhabitants, who remain fiercely proud of their inheritance and of whom some 23 per cent are Welsh-speaking. Among the mountains and valleys lie the six principal centres of population, Llanfair Caereinion, Llanfyllin, Llanidloes, Machynlleth, Newtown and Welshpool. To them must be added the former county town of Montgomery, which preserves a special entity of its own at the foot of the rock surmounted by Henry III's castle.

Many of the larger houses of the gentry have ceased to belong to their old families and are now hotels, developed often as centres for a wide range of recreational activities, e.g. golf, fishing, walking, climbing or pony trekking.

Many men and women have been reared in the area to bring distinction to their land. Among them are Robert Owen (1771–1858), Utopian socialist and founder of co-operative enterprise, David Davies (1818–1890), the self-made railway and mining industrialist and MP, and Richard Wilson who became 'the father of English landscape painting'.

Eisteddfod Powys, dating back to 1820, is now held annually within the district, while the Urdd Gobaith Cymru organises its own annual eisteddfod for the young. There is an annual festival at Llanfyllin, and that recently inaugurated at Gregynog, in the splendid residential centre of the University of Wales, is rapidly achieving international acclaim. Every area has its choir and the traditional plygain services still fill churches and chapels every year.

All these activities form a remarkable achievement for a district so comparatively sparsely populated, one indeed which has experienced a steady decline in numbers since the first half of the 19th century saw the industrialisation of South Wales with its consequent attraction of employment for those out of work elsewhere. This decline continued into much of the present century due to a sustained loss of jobs, particularly in agriculture and its related manufacturing industries. From a population of 69,000 in 1841, Montgomeryshire dropped to a little over 43,000 in 1971 despite the sudden boom in the woollen industry in the 1870s, a story which can be seen in detail in the Newtown textile museum.

Greatly as it treasures its history and its lovely surroundings, and fortunate as it is in the number of voluntary bodies existing to protect both, the district does not rest only on the past but actively strives to promote a living and up-to-date community which gives credit to its past while keeping its eyes fixed firmly on the future.

RADNORSHIRE

Radnorshire, Maesyfed in Welsh, is a county of wooded hills and narrow winding valleys where sheep, cattle and native ponies graze. It is some 36 miles long by 30 miles wide, containing 48 parishes, and is divided into the six Hundreds of Cefnllys, Colwyn, Knighton, Painscastle, Radnor and Rhayader. The greater part of the county is covered by the Registration districts of Knighton, Presteigne and Rhayader, while the Hundreds of Cefnllys and Painscastle, in the south of the county, are in the Registration districts of Builth and Hay, respectively; part of the Hundred of Radnor is in the Registration district of Kington. Almost all the Parish churches in the county are in the Diocese of St. David's, Brecon, except for a few parishes along the Hereford and Shropshire borders which are in the Diocese of Hereford.

Radnorshire, with Montgomeryshire on its north and north-west borders and Breconshire to the south and south-west form the County of Powys. To the west lie the remote uplands of Cardiganshire, where the many springs, streams and rivulets flow into the Elan Valley Reservoirs and supply water to the City of Birmingham. The River Wye marks part of the boundaries with Brecknock and Herefordshire, while the River Teme marks the boundary with Shropshire.

The many ancient tumuli, castle ruins and mounds bear witness to the turbulent history and border wars of this region during the past centuries. The area now called Radnorshire was once inhabited by the Britons and Romans but, following the Norman Conquest, the great families of Mortimer and de Breos were granted lands for their services and this caused bitter feuds with the native princes. Prince Llewellyn ap Griffith, the last of the native princes, had a hunting seat and castle at

Aberedw, where a heap of stones now marks the castle ruins and there is a small cave which is reputed to be his last hiding place.

The remote little church at Colva is thought to be the oldest church in the county and the lovely rood screen in Llananno Church is supposed to have come from the ruins of Abbey Cwmhir following its destruction by Owain Glyn Dwr in 1401.

Offa's Dyke marches along the eastern borders of the county and reminds us of past efforts to keep out marauders from over the border in early times, while Glyndwr's Way, running from Machynlleth to Pilleth, marks the route used by him and his army in their efforts to drive the English out of Wales. These two routes are now well marked trails for the many hikers who come to Radnorshire.

The Central Wales Railway linking Swansea and Shrewsbury traverses the county from Knighton in the north-east to Builth Road in the south-west. The A479 trunk road runs from Newtown in the north to Swansea in the south while the A44 links Rhayader to the industrial Midlands. Both the A479 and the railway pass through Llandrindod Wells, the administrative centre and county town of Powys, with its many hotels and elegant Victorian houses built during its heyday as a spa.

Having a wealth of lovely views and a past rich in history, Radnorshire has much to offer both tourist and scholar. The mineral springs at Llandrindod Wells, known from 1696, were so famous by 1749 that a hotel was built to accommodate the many visitors. However, the establishment became so notorious as a place of gamblers and others of ill repute that it was taken down. Two new hotels, the Pump House and the Rock House, were built nearer Rock Park and the mineral springs. To commemorate its heyday, Llandrindod Wells now holds a 'Victorian Week' annually at the end of August when the townsfolk and others are encouraged to dress in costume and decorate their shops and windows in a Victorian style. Interesting displays are mounted in the Church Hall and the Museum with the lake and adjacent play areas for the children, while visitors to Rock Park are welcome to sample the waters.

POWYS

POWYS COUNTY ARCHIVES OFFICE
County Hall, Llandrindod Wells, Powys LD1 5LG
Tel: (01597) 826088
Enquiries to the County Archivist

Opening hours

Monday   Closed
Tuesday – Thursday 10.00 a.m. – 12.30 p.m. and 1.30 p.m. – 5.00 p.m.
Friday   10.00 a.m. – 12.30 p.m. and 1.30 p.m. – 4.00 p.m.

Parking facilities

Parking is available.

Disabled facilities

There is access for wheelchairs.

Appointment system

It is necessary to make an appointment in advance.

Reader's Ticket

A CARN reader's ticket is required.

Holdings

Census returns: 1891 only

Deposited local collections, of which the following have a wider significance:

Quarter Sessions records for Breconshire, Montgomeryshire and Radnorshire

Other records of Local Government for all three counties, including parish and community councils, urban and rural district councils and county councils.

A good collection of school records.

Deeds, correspondence and related papers of Abercamlais estate, 16th–19th centuries, including correspondence and other papers of the Archdeacon Richard Davies of Brecon, late 18th–early 19th centuries.

Penybont Hall Estate; miscellaneous records, 1673–1927.

Postal queries

The archivist will respond briefly with no charge if an SAE is received.

For enquiries concerning the holdings, etc. of the records office, research enquirers are referred to independent researchers if requested.

Facilities

No refreshments available at the office.

Publications

Lists of accessions
Detailed and outline lists of individual collections
Office Guide (A4 photocopy format) price £3.00 (£4.00 by mail)

LIBRARIES

Powys County Library
Cefnllys Road, Llandrindod Wells, Powys LD1 5LD
Tel: (01597) 826087

Opening hours
Monday – Thursday   9.00 a.m. – 12.30 p.m. and 1.30 p.m. – 5.00 p.m.
Friday   9.00 a.m. – 12.30 p.m. and 1.30 p.m. – 4.00 p.m.

Brecon Area Library
Ship Street, Brecon LD3 9AE
Tel: (01874) 623346

Opening hours
Monday – Wednesday   10.00 a.m. – 5.00 p.m.
Thursday   10.00 a.m. – 7.00 p.m.
Friday   10.00 a.m. – 5.00 p.m.
Saturday   10.00 a.m. – 12.00 midday

Disabled facilities
Wheelchair access to library and to film and microfiche viewers.

Holdings
Special material covering the old County of Brecknock
Tithe maps and apportionments
Census returns on film or fiche
Newspapers on fiche include
   Brecon County Times, 1866–1933 (excluding 1897)
   Brecon Journal, approx. 1855–1868
   Brecon Reporter, approx. 1863–1867
   Silurian, 1838–1843, 1845–1848, 1849–55
   Brecon and Radnor Express, 1987 to date

Newtown Area Library
Park Lane, Newtown SY16
Tel: (01686) 626934

Opening hours
Monday, Wednesday and Thursday   9.30 a.m.–5.30 p.m.
Tuesday and Friday   9.30 a.m.–7.30 p.m.
Saturday   9.30 a.m.–12.30 p.m.

REGISTRATION OF BIRTHS, DEATHS AND MARRIAGES
Brecknock District
The Register Office
New County Hall, Glamorgan Stret, Brecon LD3 7DP
Tel: (01874) 624334

Hay District
The Register Office
Council Offices, Broad Street, Hay on Wye, via Hereford HR3 5BX
Tel: (01497) 821371

Machynlleth District
The Register Office
11 Penrallt Street, Machynlleth SY20 8AG
Tel: (01654) 702335

Mid Powys District
The Register Office
Powys County Hall, Llandrindod Wells LD1 5LE
Tel: (01597) 826373

Newtown District
The Register Office
Room 4, Council Offices, The Park, Newtown SY16 2NZ
Tel: (01686) 627862

Radnor East District
The Register Office
2 Station Road, Knighton LD7 1DU
Tel: (01547) 528332

Welshpool and Llanfyllin District
The Register Office
District Council Offices, Severn Road, WelshpoolSY21 7AS
Tel: (01938) 552828

TOURIST OFFICE
Tourist Information Centre
Old Town Hall, Temple Street, Llandrindod Wells, Powys LD1
Tel: (01597) 822600

PLACES OF INTEREST
The South Wales Borderers and Monmouthshire Regiment
Museum of the Royal Regiment of Wales, The Barracks, Brecon LD3
7EB
Tel: (01874) 623111 Ext. 2311

SOUTH WEST WALES

CARDIGANSHIRE/CEREDIGION

Cardiganshire, which in Welsh is Ceredigion, is named after Ceredig, son of Cunedda the post-Roman leader who founded it. Its long seaboard on Cardigan Bay is scattered with small villages, punctuated at either end by the towns of Cardigan and Aberystwyth. Both the towns and the villages, however small and insignificant the latter may now seem, have long histories as active ports and also, in some cases, centres of shipbuilding. The significance of this is the migration to the ports from the rural hinterland which occurred in the nineteenth century. People from as many as 27 of Cardiganshire's parishes have been found, for example, at the port of New Quay in 1851. If you have 'lost' an ancestor from an inland parish, it would pay to check the censuses at one of the ports. The remainder of the county was mainly agricultural, but there was an important lead-mining industry from the seventeenth until the twentieth centuries, which also attracted migrant workers. Those interested in the lead mines may well find help in David Bick's books: *The Old Metal Mines of Mid-Wales. Part 1: Cardiganshire South of Devil's Bridge; Part 2: The Rheidol to Goginan; Part 3: Cardiganshire North of Goginan.*

Remember, when pursuing elusive members of your family, it does pay to know local history. Rural poverty forced emigration from Cardiganshire, sometimes temporary, sometimes permanent, to the coalfields of South Wales, the men leaving home first with the families following later. Since so much of Cardiganshire was agricultural, estate records can be invaluable in tracing tenants and employees. Many of these records have been deposited at the National Library of Wales and have been calendared, that is listed with brief details of names and places for easy reference, under the name of the estate. So it pays to discover the name of the nearest 'big house' to where your ancestors lived. Many squires owned land in more than one county and some of the estate records may well be found in Carmarthen Record Office, for instance, where the Beckingsale collection has many deeds pertaining to south Cardiganshire.

Many of you will be searching for Nonconformist ancestors in Cardiganshire. There are three books which will be invaluable in this: *Cofrestri Plwyf Cymru/Parish Registers of Wales, Cofrestri Anghydffurfiol Cymru/Nonconformist Registers of Wales*, both published by the National Library of Wales, and *The Parish Churches and Nonconformist Chapels of Wales: Their records and where to find them* by Bert J. Rawlins, *Volume 1, Cardigan, Carmarthen, Pembroke*, which was published in Utah in 1987 and is available in many libraries.

CEREDIGION RECORD OFFICE

Swyddfa'r Sir Archives,
Marine Terrace, Aberystwyth, Ceredigion SY23 2DE
Tel: (01970) 633697/8

Opening hours
Monday–Friday   10.00 a.m.–4.00 p.m.

Disabled facilities
There is no easy wheelchair access and it is advisable to ring beforehand if help is needed.

Appointments
An appointment is necessary only to use the microfilm reader.

This office is the repository for the records of the former Cardiganshire County Council, and the municipal boroughs of Aberystwyth, Cardigan and Lampeter (urban and rural district councils).

Holdings
1910 valuation records for Cardiganshire, which lists owners and heads of households
Electoral registers from 1945 to the present (incomplete run)
School records, including registers of admission and school log books
Records for Petty Sessions
Ship's registers (indexed), which list some local shareholders
Census returns for Cardiganshire 1841–1891 (microfilm)
Microfiche index to the 1881 census for Cardiganshire

The original Parish Registers for Cardiganshire are at the National Library of Wales, Aberystwyth, but this office has microfilm copies of the Parish Registers with microfilm copies of some Nonconformist registers held at the PRO.

Newspapers

Cardigan and Tivyside Advertiser (1866-to date, indexed)
The Cambrian News from 1871 (incomplete)

LIBRARIES

Aberystwyth Public Library

Reference Section, Corporation Street, Aberystwyth, Ceredigion
Tel: (01970) 617464

Opening hours

Monday–Friday   9.30 a.m.–5.00 p.m.
Saturday   9.30 a.m.–1.00 p.m.

Holdings

Census returns

Aberystwyth and neighbourhood 1841–1881 (1891 has transcript and index)

North Cardiganshire Rural Districts 1841–1881

Cardigan and Lampeter 1851

1841 census Llanafan, Llanbadarn-y-Croyddin, Llanfihangel-y-Croyddin

1851 census Broncastellan and Clarach (with Llangorwen)

1841–1881 census Ysgubor-y-Coed

1841–1881 census Cwmrheidol Census Study

1841–1881 census Ceulan-y-Maesmawr, Cynnullmawr and Elerch Census study

1871 census Llanilar (transcript)

1891 census Broncastellan, Clarach, Llangawsai, Llanbadarn, Waunfawr, Pwllhoby, Vaenor Upper, Llanbadarn Croyddin Lower, Llanychaiarn (transcript and index)

1891 census Melindwr, Parcel Canol, Trefeurig (transcript and index)

1891 census for the county of Cardiganshire (microfiche)

Index of Marriages

Llanbadarn Fawr 1804–1882

St. Michael, Aberystwyth 1861–1875

Index of Baptisms

Llanbadarn Fawr 1830–1879

Tabernacle, Aberystwyth; Ponterwyd Calvinistic Methodist; Trisant Calvinistic Methodist.

Index of Burials

Llanbadarn Fawr 1830–1879

St. Michael, Aberystwyth 1813–1879 (alphabetical transcript of the burials register)

Index of tombstone memorials for St. Michael's Churchyard, Aberystwyth

Also available

Trade Directories issued in past years (no current volumes)

Press cuttings from local newspapers over 25 years in Cardiganshire

Parish histories for Cardiganshire, some translated from the original Welsh (Local History Section)

Cardiganshire pictures and slides

Audio tapes of the reminiscences of local people

REGISTRATION OF BIRTHS, DEATHS AND MARRIAGES

Ceredigion, North

County Hall, Aberystwyth, Ceredigion SY23 2DE

Ceredigion, Central

21 High Street, Lampeter, Ceredigion SA48 7BH

Ceredigion, South

Glyncoed Chambers, Priory Street

Cardigan, Ceredigion SA43 1BX

CEREDIGION TOURIST INFORMATION CENTRES

Aberystwyth   Tel: (01970) 612125

Cardigan   Tel: (01239) 613230

CARMARTHENSHIRE

The story of Carmarthenshire has something to interest everyone, from the Romans to the Rebecca Riots, from centuries of thriving ports to the discovery of tinplate.

Carmarthen itself was called Maridunum by the Romans but in Welsh it is Caerfyrddin, which is said to suggest that this was the place of Myrddin, Merlin the magician. The town was a flourishing port from early times and there are records of trade in wool and hides from before the 16th century. It was important in coastal and foreign trade even though there were continual problems with the silting of the River Towy.

In the early 19th century there were 51 vessels registered as belonging to the port but the coming of the railways reduced the sea traffic. The South Wales Railway reached Carmarthen in 1852 and several of the railways which were built in the second half of the 19th century used the three stations in the town. This meant that the men and women of Carmarthenshire were able to travel in their thousands to the industries developing in the south east of the county around Llanelli and still further to Glamorgan and Monmouthshire.

If there are researchers who find their families in the parishes of Llanfair-ar-y-bryn or Myddfai in the north east of the county at the end of the 18th or the beginning of the 19th centuries, it is very likely that they had been drawn there to work in the lead mines. Workers moved in from rural Breconshire and judging by the surnames, such as Bathesby, Sachary and Silkstone which appear in the Parish Registers, many had come much further.

South-east Carmarthenshire saw protest in the early 19th century, which was a time of great rural hardship. When Turnpike Trusts set up illegal tollgates, groups of men dressed in women's clothes turned out to destroy them. They became known as Rebecca and her daughters and it is said that the name originated from a verse from Genesis which was heard during the disturbances

> 'And they blessed Rebecca, and said unto her, Thou art our sister. Be thou the mother of thousands of millions, and let thy seed possess the gate of they that hate them.'

The Gwendraeth and Amman coalfield was late joining the Industrial Revolution as the anthracite produced was a slow combustion coal, but with developments in blasting equipment the whole area became industrialized. Llanelli began to grow in the 1850s and attracted workers from all over south-west Wales. It became an important centre for the manufacture of tinplate in which sheets of iron or steel were coated with very thin layers of tin. This was exported far and wide, with America an important customer, as cans were needed in the food processing plants. Llanelli, which had developed so quickly, declined just as quickly in the 1960s.

From this glimpse of the turbulent and interesting history of Carmarthenshire it is obvious that it has not always been the peaceful county that it is now.

CARMARTHENSHIRE RECORD OFFICE

County Hall, Carmarthen, Carmarthenshire SA31 1JP
Tel: (01267) 224184

Opening hours

Monday	9.00 a.m.–7.00 p.m.
Tuesday–Thursday	9.00 a.m.–4.45 p.m.
Friday	9.00 a.m.–4.15 p.m.

Car parking

There is limited parking in the County Hall car park.

Disabled facilities

Disabled access is available at the back of the County Hall.

Holdings

The Public Records which are held include:

Ecclesiastical records of the Church in Wales; the Nonconformist non-parochial registers held in the Public Record Office on microfilm; some original chapel records 18th - 20th century

Electoral Registers

Land Tax 1797

Hearth Tax 1670

Survey of Crown lands 1560

Carmarthenshire Quarter Sessions and Petty Sessions

Official records of Carmarthenshire County Council and the Borough records of Carmarthen, Kidwelly, Laugharne and Llandovery.

1881 census for the county of Carmarthenshire with index

A large proportion of the archives held by the Carmarthenshire Record Office are deposited records, that is records belonging to individuals or organisations which the owners have placed in the Record Office for safe-keeping, such as the large estate collections. These include collections for

Cawdor, Dynevor, Mansel-Lewis, Cynghordy,
Derwydd, Stepney, Aberglasney, Plas Llanstephan
and many more.

A leaflet with further information on holdings is available.

Postal research

The Archivist will respond to limited postal queries without charge.

LIBRARIES

Carmarthen Library

St. Peters Street, Carmarthen, Carmarthenshire
(opposite St.Peters Church)
Tel: (01267) 224822 or 230873

Opening hours

Mondays–Fridays   10.00 a.m.–7.00 p.m.
Saturday   10.00 a.m.–1.00 p.m.

Car parking

There is a large municipal car park 50 yards away.

Disabled facilities

There is no wheelchair access to the Reference Library but the Librarian would set up reader and film in the Lending Library, on a lower floor, by appointment.

Appointments

An appointment for the use of film readers is recommended.

Holdings

Census Returns for the whole of Carmarthenshire 1841–1891 (1861 is not complete as some parishes were missing when the returns went to the PRO, e.g. St. Clears and Laugharne)
Newspapers on microfilm
   Carmarthen Journal from 1810 (some subjects indexed)
   Carmarthen Times/Citizen from 1962
   Celtic News/Cymric Times 1923–1935
   The Cambrian 1804–1812
   The Welshman 1832–1945
   The Amman Valley Chronicle from 1913
Some histories of individual families and translations from the original Welsh of the histories of Nonconformist chapels of the County, written by their ministers.

Local History

Carmarthen Museum, Abergwili, Carmarthen SA31 2JG

Llanelli Public Library

Vaughan Street, Llanelli, Carmarthenshire SA15 3AS
Tel: (01554) 773538
Fax: (01554) 750125

Reference Library opening hours

Monday, Thursday and Friday	9.30 a.m.–7.00 p.m.
Tuesday and Wednesday	9.30 a.m.–6.00 p.m.
Saturday	9.30 a.m.–5.00 p.m.

Car parking

Public car park opposite the library.

Facilities

There are no toilets.

Disabled facilities

There is no disabled access.

Holdings

The library has collections on local matters with special emphasis on the coal industry and tinplate making.

The main collections available are:

Llanelli Harbour Trust records

The Neville Industrial Records (microfilm); an excellent source of information on the copper industry.

The Stepney Estate collection, original deeds, etc.

The Library also holds:

1841–1891 census for the Llanelli area (can be photocopied)

Llanelli newspapers 1863 onwards (indexed 1863–1988)

Llanelli and County Guardian 1863–1926 Indexed (in detail with Births, Marriages and Deaths)

Postal queries

Short queries will be answered (e.g. checking an exact address in the census). Longer enquiries will be charged at the following rates

15–30 minutes	£10.00 (incl. VAT)
30–60 minutes	£20.00 (incl. VAT)
Over 60 minutes	£20.00 + £5.00 (incl. VAT) for every additional 15 minutes.

Llandeilo Fawr Library

Crescent Road, Llandeilo Fawr, Carmarthenshire SA19 6HN
(Located at the top end of the car park.)
Tel: (01558) 823659

Opening hours

Tuesday, Friday	10.00 a.m.–12.00 noon, 1.30 p.m.–4.30 p.m., 5.00 p.m.–7.00 p.m.
Wednesday	1.30 p.m.–5.00 p.m.
Saturday	10.00 a.m.–12.00 noon

Disabled facilities

There is wheelchair access.

Holdings

The library holds books in print of local interest and box files with items of recent and historical interest.

REGISTRATION OF BIRTHS, DEATHS AND MARRIAGES

Carmarthen and the county (except Llanelli)

Jeremy's Buildings, St. Peters Street, Carmarthen, Carmarthenshire SA31 1LN

Llanelli

County Council Offices, Swansea Road, Llanelli, Carmarthenshire SA15 3DJ

CARMARTHENSHIRE TOURIST INFORMATION SERVICE

Carmarthen (Lammas Street)

Tel: (01267) 231557

Llanelli (Branch Library, Vaughan Street)

Tel: (01554) 772020

THE CHURCH OF JESUS CHRIST OF LATTER-DAY SAINTS

Family History Centre,
Cardigan Road, Newcastle Emlyn, Carmarthenshire
Tel: (01559) 370945

This centre was opened recently and is part of the new church of Jesus Christ of Latter-day Saints.

Opening hours

Wednesdays and Fridays   6.00 p.m.–10.00 p.m.

Appointments

It is necessary to book in advance to use one of the microfiche readers and a donation is requested.

Charges

There is an hourly charge for the use of the computer and it is possible to update research material from it.

Holdings

The research material available at present includes
1992 I.G.I.
1881 census for England and Wales, with the exception of Surrey, Middlesex and Kent
Most of Boyd's Marriage Index 1538–1837.
There are plans to increase these resources when funds allow.

PEMBROKESHIRE

Pembrokeshire, the most westerly county of Wales, was known as Demetia, or Dyfed, in Roman times. When the counties of Wales were first formed in the 16th century, Pembrokeshire already existed as a county palatine, the only one in Wales. The inhabitants of a county palatine obeyed their Earl before the king himself.

With its gently undulating hills and fertile valleys rising to the Preseli Hills, its sea coast is double that of its land boundary; to the north is the sea and the south-west corner of Cardiganshire, to the east is Carmarthenshire and to the south and west Bristol and St. George's Channel. Geologically it is very interesting and some of the oldest rocks in the world can be found within its boundaries.

Its people are an amalgam of Vikings, Normans, Flemings, English, Irish and, of course, Welsh. Many surnames found in the Registers are peculiar to Pembrokeshire. It is unique in Wales because it has a linguistic divide called The Landsker which divides the Welsh speaking north from the English speaking south. This dates from the 11th century when the Normans built a frontier of castles and strongholds, known as the Landsker, across the county to protect their lands. The influence of its people has spread far and wide, not least as followers of Strongbow, when he conquered Ireland, and later as workers in the South Wales Valleys during the Industrial Revolution.

Some of the towns in the county are among the oldest in Wales and there is evidence that the Norsemen established a trading post at Haverfordwest with the Normans building castles and earthworks in several places. Pembroke Dock, however, was a 'new town', built in 1814. It is said that Nelson himself approved the site on Milford Haven so that the extra ships needed for the war against France could be constructed. Builders from many parts of the country worked on the town which is laid out in a grid pattern, with wide streets.

Pembrokeshire's two main industries for generations have been based on fishing and agriculture. Today its fishing fleets have dwindled and the world famous natural harbour of Milford Haven is more famous for its oil industry than its ship building. There was a time when a thriving coal mining industry existed in a wide band running from Nolton Haven to Saundersfoot, when lead and slate were mined in the north with scattered pockets of other minerals, but those days have gone. However, it still retains its lovely countryside, sandy beaches and windswept cliffs, where its friendly, cosmopolitan people welcome thousands of holidaymakers every year to share in its beauty.

PEMBROKESHIRE RECORD OFFICE

The Castle, Haverfordwest, Pembrokeshire SA61 2EF

Tel: (01437) 763707

Opening hours

Monday–Thursday   9.00 a.m.–4.45 p.m.
Friday   9.00 a.m.–4.15 p.m.
First Saturday in the month
   (not Bank Holiday weekends)   9.30 a.m.–12.30 p.m.
No Reader's ticket is required.

Appointments

No appointment is necessary to use the Reading Room.

Car parking

Parking is available.

Disabled facilities

Wheel chair access available.

Holdings

A summary of the main collections is given here but a detailed list is available on request.

Quarter Sessions of Pembrokeshire and Haverfordwest
Shipping Records: Port of Cardigan(1824–1856)
                            Port of Milford (1827–1930)
Copies of some Nonconformist registers held in the PRO (late 18th–20th centuries)
Registers of baptisms, marriages and burials for about 80 Anglican parishes, with microfilm copies of others.
Census returns for the county of Pembroke on microfilm (1881 indexed)
Some deposited family and estate collections

Postal queries

One initial query will be answered without charge then a list of researchers will be offered.

LIBRARIES AND MUSEUMS

Haverfordwest Public Library

Dew Street, Haverfordwest, Pembrokeshire SA61 1SU

Tel: (01437) 764591/762070 Ext. 5248 for Reference Library

Opening hours

Monday, Wednesday and Thursday	9.30 a.m.–5.00 p.m.
Tuesday and Friday	9.30 a.m.–7.00 p.m.
Saturday	9.30 a.m.–1.00 p.m.

Disabled facilities

Unfortunately there is no wheel chair access to the Library as the Reference and Local Studies Department is up two flights of stairs on the first floor.

Holdings

Reference books, containing general information on surnames, heraldry, tracing your family, peerages, etc.

Local studies, a multi-format collection (including books, newscuttings etc.) relating to people, places and events within Pembrokeshire. It contains many family histories, trade directories, electoral registers, etc. There is a card index to this collection.

Newspapers

The Pembrokeshire Herald 1844–1909 (microfilm)

The Western Telegraph 1975 to date

The West Wales Guardian 1975 to date

I.G.I. 1992 edition (microfiche)

Family Search (includes the I.G.I.), 1994 edition on CD ROM

The Francis Green Collection. Francis Green was a prominent local historian working at the turn of the century. He transcribed many documents (wills, muster books, plea rolls, obituaries, marriage licences, etc.) relating to the genealogies of the leading families of Cardiganshire, Carmarthenshire and Pembrokeshire as well as documents which name a great many people of the area. These are organised into

(1) 35 volumes of Wills with notes,

(2) approximately 800 sheet pedigrees of families,

(3) Parish Registers for Cardiganshire, Carmarthenshire, Pembrokeshire and Glamorgan, and

(4) booklets relating to Pembrokeshire genealogy.

There is a card index to the collection.

TENBY MUSEUM

Castle Hill, Tenby, Pembrokeshire SA70 7BP

Tel: (01834) 842809

Opening hours

Easter–October 31st

Daily, including Sunday 10.00 a.m.–6.00 p.m.

November 1st–Easter

Weekdays   10.00 a.m.–4.00 p.m.

Entry charge

Adults	£1.20
Students and OAPs	80p
Children	60p
Families	£3.00

Disabled facilities

There is no specific disabled access due to site restraints.

Research facilities

Research facilities are available on application to the Curator.

Holdings

Copy archives available are:

1851, 1871 and 1881 transcribed censuses

1928–1971 Burial Register for St.Mary's Church, together with a survey of the graves in Tenby Cemetery, carried out in 1974

Electors Lists for Tenby for 1853, 1871, 1889, 1939, 1945 and 1954, plus all up-to date lists

Large number of original copies of *The Tenby Observer* and *The West Wales Guardian*

Various papers collected by the late Judge Edgerton Allen on 'Old Welsh families', which include Adams, Allen, Barrett, Bowen, Childs, Stokes and the Warren families

Various books on established Pembrokeshire families

SUPERINTENDENT REGISTRARS

Haverfordwest

Tower Hill, Haverfordwest, Pembrokeshire SA61 1SR

Tel: Births and Deaths   (01437) 763543

Marriages   (01437) 762597

Pembroke and District
East Back, Pembroke, Pembrokeshire SA71 4HL
Tel: Marriages only   (01646) 682432

TOURIST INFORMATION CENTRES, PEMBROKESHIRE
Haverfordwest (Old Bridge)   Tel: (01437) 763110
Tenby (The Croft)   Tel: (01834) 842402

INFORMATION ON SOUTH PEMBROKESHIRE
Information is available from
South Pembrokeshire Partnership for Action with Rural Communities
   (SPARC)
c/o The Old School, Station Road
Narberth, Pembrokeshire SA67 8DU
Tel: (01834) 860965
Visitors' guides and holiday suggestions, together with a list of leaflets giving the history of many of the villages in this area, are available from the above address.

GLAMORGAN

Glamorgan, covering 813 square miles of land, is situated in the South Eastern part of Wales. It is bounded by water to some degree on all four sides; the Bristol Channel on the south, the River Rhymney to the east, Rhossily Bay and the River Lougher to the west, with the northern boundary made up of four smaller rivers, Twrch, Pyrddin, Sychant and Cynon. About a third of the area is heath land, forests and mountains rising to 1,969 feet.

Cardiff is the main town and also the capital city of the Principality of Wales; together with Swansea, Port Talbot and Barry it is one of the main ports of the Bristol Channel. The Bristol Channel has the second highest tide in the world, but it is only safe for ships to dock one hour each side of high tide, because of the mud and silt which comes down from the rivers.

Quite early in the 18th century an iron works was established at Cyfarthfa, Merthyr Tydfil, where water and timber were plentiful, for at that time it was charcoal, not coal, which was used for smelting. This works and another at Dowlais drew thousands of migrant workers to Merthyr from all over the British Isles during the industrial boom which followed. Many researchers will find that their ancestors spent part, if not all, of their lives in the crowded conditions of 19th century Merthyr.

During the industrial boom all the iron and coal produced in Merthyr Tydfil and the Welsh Valleys had to be transported to the docks but expansion was limited then by the difficulty of taking the pig iron to the port of Cardiff. It was in 1794 that the 'Glamorgan Canal' was opened. The 26 miles of the canal and the 50 locks were dug by teams of navigators, usually called 'navvies'; it had a fall of 600 feet. In 1836, as railways began to replace canals, the 'Taff Vale Railway' was opened in the valley with a branch line to Aberdare. It followed roughly the same path as the River Taff and the canal from Merthyr Tydfil, but at the junction in Pontypridd it picked up further supplies of minerals from the Rhondda Valley. In the 1830s and 1840s the ports had to be enlarged to accommodate the extra trade, for at one time Cardiff was exporting coal to all corners of the world.

This period brought a population explosion which changed Glamorgan beyond all recognition. From being mainly farmers and their workers speaking Welsh, the majority of the population became industrial workers in the collieries and iron works where other languages besides Welsh and English were heard. This was to see the demise of the Welsh language in the area and now Welsh is spoken only in small pockets around the county.

There were changes, too, in the religion of the people, for Non-conformity came with the Baptists, Methodists and Wesleyans, the latter due to the famous Wesley brothers who stayed at Fonmon Castle with Robert Jones.

It could be said that Glamorgan was changed by the Industrial Revolution more than any other county in Wales. Thousands of workers poured in from all parts of the British Isles and beyond. These people had the courage to leave their own villages and adapt to the demands of the new life. Glamorgan still shows signs of their enterprise.

In April 1996 Local Authority changes came into effect in Wales and Glamorgan has become eight authorities, seven borough councils and the County of Swansea, which are listed at the end of this book. However, the names of the towns remain the same so all the information which is listed here still applies.

GLAMORGAN RECORD OFFICE

Mid-Glamorgan County Hall, Cathays Park Cardiff CF1 3NE
Tel: (01222) 780282
Family History Search Room Tel: (01222) 780285

Opening hours

Monday	Closed
Tuesday and Thursday	9.00 a.m.–1.00 p.m. and 2.00 p.m.–5.00 p.m.
Wednesday	Open until 7.00 p.m. by appointment if made before 4.00 p.m.
Friday	4.00 p.m. closing

Car parking

No car parking is available.

Disabled facilities
Facilities are available if notice is given in advance.

Appointments
It is necessary to book film and fiche readers in advance.

Charges
A charge of 50p per half hour is made for the use of film and fiche readers.

Holdings

Census returns	All county 1841–1881
	Mid- and South Glamorgan for 1891
	Complete index for West Monmouthshire and Glamorgan 1851–1881
Parish Registers	Llandaff diocesan parishes
Bishop's Transcripts	Llandaff diocesan parishes (microfilm)
St Catherine's House Indexes	1837–1980
Somerset House Indexes	1858–1950

Postal research
A charge of £15 per hour is made.

THE CITY AND COUNTY OF SWANSEA ARCHIVES SERVICE
County Hall, Oystermouth Road, County of Swansea SA1 3SN
Tel: (01792) 636589

Opening hours
Monday–Thursday 9.00 a.m.–5.30 p.m.
Monday only   5.30 p.m.–7.30 p.m. by appointment

Car parking
Car parking is available.

Disabled facilities
There are facilities for the disabled.

Appointments
An appointment is necessary to use the microfilm reader.

Charges
There is a charge of 50p per half hour for film and fiche readers.

Holdings
Census returns for Glamorgan and parts of Monmouthshire 1841–1891

Census name indexes for Gower 1841
Glamorgan 1851
England and Wales 1881
Margam 1891
St. Catherine's House Indexes 1837–1983
I.G.I. for Great Britain and Ireland, 1992 edition
Probate Registry Indexes St. Davids 1564–1858
Llandaff 1753–1857
Archdeaconry Court of Brecon 1557–1858
Archdeaconry Court of Carmarthen 1600–1858
Parish Registers   West Glamorgan
Bishop's Transcripts   West Glamorgan, 17th century–1858
Glamorgan Family History Society Indexes
Shipping records, including crew agreements, for the ports of Swansea and Port Talbot 1863–1913
Welsh casualty list for the South African War 1899–1902
Hearth Tax returns for Glamorgan, 1670–1672

Postal research

A charge of £15 per hour is made.

Facilities

Readers may use the County Hall snack bar.

Publications

Tracing Your Family History–A Beginner's Guide

SWANSEA CITY ARCHIVES

The Guildhall, Swansea SA1 4PE
Tel: (01792) 302126
Fax: (01792) 467432

Opening hours

Tuesday and Wednesday 9.30 a.m.–12.45 p.m. and 2.15 p.m.–4.30 p.m.
An appointment is necessary to consult documents at any other time.

Holdings

Documents pertaining to the City/Town rate books from 1846
Electoral registers from 1867

LIBRARIES

Barry Library

Kings Square, Barry, South Glamorgan
Tel: (01446) 735722
Closed Thursdays

Holdings

Extensive collection of local newspapers from 1890.

Bridgend Library

Mid-Glamorgan County Library HQ, Coed Parc, Park Street, Bridgend,
Mid-Glamorgan CF31 4BA
Tel: (01656) 767451

Opening hours

Monday	9.00 a.m.–5.00 p.m.
Tuesday and Thursday	8.30 a.m.–5.00 p.m.
Friday	8.30 a.m.–4.30 p.m.

Cardiff Central Library

St.David's Link, Frederick Street, Cardiff, South Glamorgan
Tel: (01222) 382116

Opening hours

Monday and Tuesday	9.30 a.m.–6.00 p.m.
Wednesday and Thursday	9.00 a.m.–8.00 p.m.
Friday	9.00 a.m.–6.00 p.m.
Saturday	9.00 a.m.–5.30 p.m.

For other libraries in South Glamorgan, enquire at Cardiff Library.

Pontypridd Library

Library Road, Pontypridd CF37 2DY
Tel: (01443) 486850

Holdings

Extensive local history section.

Merthyr Tydfil Public Libraries

High Street, Merthyr Tydfil, Mid-Glamorgan CF47 8AN
Tel: (01685) 723057

Opening hours

Monday–Friday	9.00 a.m.–6.00 p.m.
Saturday	9.00 a.m.–12.00 noon

Publications

The Unconquerable Spirit—Merthyr and District in the 1930s, a series of booklets using old photographs of Merthyr.

Book 1:   *Valley Views. Historic Street Scenes of Merthyr Tydfil"*
Book 2:   *Transport. Historic Scenes of the Merthyr Tydfil Valley*
Book 3:   *Industrial Life of the Valley.*

The County Borough of Merthyr Tydfil, compiled to celebrate the return of Merthyr to County Borough status.

Information on prices can be obtained from the Librarian.

Dowlais Library

Dowlais, Merthyr Tydfil

Opening hours

Monday—Friday   9.00 a.m.—6.00 p.m.
Saturday   9.00 a.m.—12.00 noon

Holdings

Parish registers for Dowlais Parish Church.

Rhondda Borough Council, Libraries Department

Treorchy Central Library, Station Road, Treorchy
Tel: (01443) 773204

Opening hours

Monday—Thursday   9.30 a.m.—5.15 p.m.
Friday   1.00 p.m.—8.00 p.m.
Saturday   9.00 a.m.—12.00 noon

Holdings

Local History material available at Treorchy Library.
   Census Returns for the years 1841, 1851, 1861, 1871, 1881, and 1891 for Ystradyfodwg Parish, Llanwonno (part containing Rhondda Fach), Llantrisant (Cymer Porth and Dinas, etc.)
Local newspapers available (microfilm)
   Rhondda Leader, 1897—1943 (1944—1991 bound in volumes)
   South Wales Echo, 1848 to date
   Western Mail, 1987 to date
Burial records for four public cemeteries (microfilm)
   Treorchy Cemetery,December 1887—May 1988, 59,935 burials
   Trealaw Cemetery,April 1881—July 1990, 72,078 burials
      The Trealaw records include burials of miners killed in the Dinas pit explosion on the 13th January 1879 but were buried

intermittently as late as November 1882. These records give the name of the deceased, occupation if male adult, otherwise relationship to the head of the family, the place the death occurred, i.e. could be the name of the pit or later in hospital, the minister's name and grave reference.

Penrhys Cemetery,May 1927–June 1991, 11,561 burials

Ferndale Cemetery,May 1877–June 1991, 16,425 burials

Other records include:

Tithe Apportionment (1847) for Llantrisant, Llanwonno, and Ystradyfodwg

Ynysfach Baptist Church Register 1795–1849

Nebo Baptists and marriages

Glynrhonthey Manorial Records (2 reels)

Miskin Manor Records (3 reels)

Ystradyfodwg Local Board Minute books November 1877–1891

Lordship of Glamorgan (a) Rolls 1–18, (b) Ministers accounts

Llanwonno and Ystradyfodwg Church Records 1717–1907

Leases, Dunraven Estate

Diaries of William Southern Clark for 1847, 1849, 1850, January 1854–November 1855

A History of the Parish of Ystradyfodwg, 1902

Ocean and National Magazine, Vol. 1 (1928)–Vol. 13 (1940)

I.G.I. for England and Wales, 1984 (microfiche)

Incomplete set of Trade Directories

Aberdare Central Library

Tel: (01685) 878888

Holdings

The following material is available for research purposes

Census returns:

1841 Aberdare, Llanwonno, part of Ystradyfodwg (Rhondda), Rhigos, Pontwelby, Llantrisant, Llanwit Fardre, Pentyrch, Radyr, Penderyn

1851 Aberdare, Llanwonno, Llanfabon, Gelligaer, Penderyn

1861 Aberdare, Llanwonno, Part of Rhondda, Penderyn

1871 Aberdare, Llanwonno, Llanfabon (part), Penderyn

1881 Aberdare, Llanwonno, Llanfabon (part), part of Rhondda, Penderyn

1891 Aberdare, Penderyn, Rhondda and Llanwonno (fiche)

Local Newspapers (microfilm)
    Cardiff and Merthyr Guardian, 1842–1874
    Y Gwron Cymreig, 1852–1860
    Mountain Ash Post, 1912–1920
    Glamorgan, Monmouth and Brecon Gazette, 1833–1841
    Aberdare Times, 1861–1902
    Aberdare Leader, 1902 to date
    Mountain Ash Leader, 1902 to date
    Y Gwron, 1856–1860

The W. W. Price and R. Ivor Parry Collection
    A general index can be consulted at the library. The collection
    includes local government and parish records, transcripts, sales
    catalogues, chapel histories. The biographical section includes a 30
    volume index to about 40,000 entries with details of the lives of
    anyone who was of wider note in the district.

Other material includes:
    Bishop's Transcripts for Aberdare 1717–1851 (microfilm)
    Transcripts of Aberdare Parish Records 1734–1890 (indexed)
    Parish Magazines for various local churches from 1882
    Hearth Tax Returns for Aberdare
    Religious Census of March 1851
    Tithe maps and Schedules for the Parishes of Penderyn (1840),
    Llanwonno (1842), and Aberdare (1844)
    An excellent set of old Ordnance Survey 25 in. maps covering most
    of the old parishes of Aberdare and Llanwonno as they were in
    1874/75
    Monumental Inscriptions for some chapels

The Mid-Glamorgan Library Service

The following facilities are available
    Newspapers include *Western Mail, Pontypridd Observer,* and
    Rhymney Valley Express
    Census enumerators' books (microfilm)
    Tithe maps and apportionments (1840s) for every Mid-Glamorgan
    parish
    I.G.I. (1988) for Great Britain
    Ordnance survey maps from 1833 to the present day
    Photographs
    School and Parish magazines
    H.M.I. reports on local schools

Oral History recordings
Directories, e.g. Kelly's and Websters
Manuscript collections of prominent local historians

The County of Swansea Library Service

Three major local history collections are housed at Neath, Port Talbot and Swansea Reference Libraries. The largest and oldest collection is at Swansea Reference Library.

Swansea Central Reference Library

Alexandra Road, Swansea
Tel: (01792) 655521 and 654065

Opening hours

Monday–Wednesday and Friday	9.00 a.m.–7.00 p.m.
Thursday and Saturday	9.00 a.m.–5.00 p.m.

Holdings

I.G.I.
1841–1881 census returns for Swansea
1891 census returns for West Glamorgan
Trade Directories
Local Newspapers
The Times from 1785 (incomplete)
Electoral Registers and Burgess Lists
Ordnance Survey and Tithe Maps
Local telephone directories from 1904

The local history collection includes:

(a) Books, directories, guides, reports, council minutes, electoral registers and periodicals.
(b) The Dylan Thomas Collection consists of over 3000 books and articles by, or about, the Swansea-born poet and author.
(c) Newspapers include the *Cambrian* from 1804 and *South Wales Evening Post* from 1893.
(d) Illustrations and prints, old and modern photographs, postcards, etc.
(e) Maps and plans from 1850.
(f) Newspapers and census returns on microfilm.

Neath Library

Victoria Gardens, Neath
Tel: (01639) 644604 and 635017

Opening hours

Monday–Wednesday, Friday   9.30 a.m.–12.30 p.m., 1.30 p.m.–5.30 p.m.
Thursday and Saturday   9.30 a.m.–12.30 p.m., 1.30 p.m.–5.00 p.m.

Holdings

1891 census returns for the Neath area and some hard copy of other census returns
Neath Guardian from 1927

Taibach Library (Port Talbot)

Commercial Road, Taibach, Port Talbot
Tel: (01639) 884521 and 883831

Opening hours

Monday–Friday   9.30 a.m.–1.00 p.m. and 2.00 p.m.–5.30 p.m.
Saturday   9.30 a.m.–1.00 p.m. and 2.00 p.m.–5.00 p.m.

Holdings

Local Newspapers
1891 Census returns for the local area
1881 Census returns for Margam and Aberavon
Some hard copy of 1841–1871 census returns

UNIVERSITY LIBRARIES

University Library, University of Wales

Singleton Park, Swansea
Tel: (01792) 295697

Opening hours

During term
   Monday–Friday   9.00 a.m.–10.00 p.m.
   Saturday   9.00 a.m.–5.00 p.m.
During vacation
   Monday–Friday   9.00 a.m.–5.00 p.m.
   Saturday   9.00 a.m.–12.00 noon

Holdings

Records include
   Limited I.G.I. and census returns for the local area
   The Times newspaper and indexes
   The Charters of Swansea and other records of the history of the town deposited before the City archives opened in 1974
   Indexes to PCC wills
   Publications of various County Record Societies
   Local Catholic church records

Arts and Social Studies Library, University of Wales, Cardiff
Cathays Park, Cardiff CF1 3XT
Tel: (01222) 874795
Fees
The joining fee is £25.00.
Two passport photographs and identification are also required.

REGISTRATION OF BIRTHS, DEATHS AND MARRIAGES

Since the new local authorities came into being on April 1st 1996 there have been changes in the Register offices of the old county of Glamorgan as the Registrars begin the task of moving registers to the areas now covered by their office. Anyone who wants to locate and order a certificate in the Cardiff area is advised to ring the offices to establish the whereabouts of the registers they need before sending any money.

Bridgend
The Register Office
County Council Offices, Sunnyside, Bridgend. CF31 4AR
Tel: (01656) 766211

Vale of Glamorgan (for the Barry area)
The Register Office
2–6 Holton Road, Barry CF63 4HD
Registers for the Vale from 1837. This now includes Cowbridge but registers for Cowbridge 1837–1874 are still in Bridgend (1996).

Caerphilly
The Register Office
Council Offices, Ystrad Fawr, Ystrad Mynach, Hengoed CF8 7SF
Tel: (01443) 863478
Registers for the parishes of Eglwysilian and Gelligaer.

Cardiff
The Register Office
48 Park Place, Cardiff
Tel: (01222) 871690

Merthyr Tydfil
The Register Office
4th Floor, Oldway House, Castle Street, Merthyr Tydfil CF47 8JB
Tel: (01685) 723318

The Register Office for Merthyr Tydfil is open on Monday, Wednesday and Friday mornings and Tuesday and Thursday afternoons only.

Pontypridd

The Superintendent Registrar
District Register Office, Court House Street, Pontypridd CF37 1JS
Tel: (01443) 486869
Includes Llantrisant registers of Births and Deaths.

Neath

The Register Office
119 London Road, Neath, Neath and Port Talbot CB SA11 1HL
Tel: (01639) 643696

Swansea

The Superintendent Registrar
County Hall, The County of Swansea SA1 3SN
Tel: (01792) 636188

TOURIST OFFICES

Cardiff Central Station
Tel: (01222) 227281

Singleton Street, Swansea SA1 3QN
Tel: (01792) 468321

Oystermouth Square, Mumbles, Swansea SA3 4DQ
Tel: (01792) 361302

THE CHURCH OF JESUS CHRIST OF LATTER-DAY SAINTS, FAMILY HISTORY CENTRES

The Church of Jesus Christ of Latter-day Saints Family History Centre, Cardiff CF4 6UH

The Church is located in Rhiwbina, at the junction of Heol-y-Deri, and Heol-Llanishen Fach.

Tel: (01222) 625342

Opening hours

Monday   10.00 a.m.–4.00 p.m.
Tuesday and Wednesday 10.00 a.m.–4.00 p.m. and 7.00 p.m.–9.00 p.m.
Thursday and Friday   1.00 p.m.–6.00 p.m. and 7.00 p.m–9.00 p.m.

Car parking

There is ample car parking at the rear of the building. Access to the Centre is by the rear door adjacent to the car park.

Appointments

The use of the centre's facilities can be arranged by prior appointment. Telephone only during the above times.

Holdings

Population Census for 1891. Complete for England and Wales

Indexed census for 1881 as published for England and Wales, some for Scotland

Some christenings and marriages for Scotland (microfiche)

Boyd's Marriage Index (microfiche)

Author titles

Locality catalogue (microfiche)

St. Catherine's House Indexes (microfilm) includes
  marriages and deaths from 1837 to 1903
  births from 1837 to 1906

Some census records for England and Wales from 1841 to 1881

Some church records for England and Wales

Any Census or Church records which are not immediately available can be ordered. The following charges are made for ordering and the subsequent hire.

£2.55 for 4 weeks hire

£3.65 for 12 weeks hire

£4.40 for an indefinite period

These records must be read at the centre.

Facilities

We would respectfully remind patrons that the drinking of tea, coffee or other beverages, and smoking are not allowed on the church premises.

The Church of Jesus Christ of Latter-day Saints Family History Centre, Merthyr Tydfil

The Librarian, Church of Latter-day Saints,
Nantygwenith Street, Georgetown, Merthyr Tydfil CF48 1NR
Tel: (01685) 722455

Appointments

For details, see LDS information for Cardiff, above.

The Church of Jesus Christ of Latter-day Saints Family History Centre, Swansea

Cockett Road, Swansea
Tel: (01792) 580110

Appointments
For details, see LDS information for Cardiff, above.

MARINE SAFETY AGENCY

Registry of Shipping and Seamen
Anchor House, Cheviot Close
Unit 5, Parc Ty Glas, Llanishen, Cardiff CF4 5JA
Tel: (01222) 747333
Fax: (01222) 747877

Holdings
Seamen's service records, 1939–1972
Masters and Mates, from 1965 to date
Crew lists and agreements, 1939–1950 and 1970 to date
Births and deaths at sea, 1891 to date
Marriages at sea, 1857 to date
Medals. Records of medals awarded to Merchant seamen
  First World War
  Second World War
  Korean war
The majority of the above information is available by post and involves a search fee.

PLACES OF INTEREST IN AND AROUND CARDIFF

Welsh Folk Museum

Museum of Welsh Life, St. Fagans, Cardiff CF5 6XB
Tel: (01222) 569441

Welsh Industrial and Maritime Museum

Bute Street, Cardiff
Tel: (01222) 481919

The Welch Regiment Museum

Cardiff Castle, Duke Street, Cardiff CF1 2RB
Tel: (01222) 229367

1st The Queens Dragoon Guards

Regimental Museum, Cardiff Castle, Duke Street, Cardiff CF1 2RB
Tel: (01222) 222253

South Wales Police Museum
Bridgend CF31 3SU
Tel: (01656) 655555

PLACES OF INTEREST IN SWANSEA

The South Wales Miners' Library
Hendrefoelan House, Gower Road, Swansea SA2 7NB
Tel: (01792) 201231 Ext. 2003
This library was established by the University College of Wales in Swansea in 1973 to house material collected by the Coalfield History Project. The collection includes photographs, posters, lodge banners, oral history tapes and a wide variety of books rescued from miners' institute libraries.

Opening hours
Monday–Friday 9.00 a.m.–1.00 p.m. and 2.00 p.m.–5.00 p.m.
for research and browsing. The staff are always pleased to show researchers around or help with enquiries.

Holdings
South Wales Miners' Federation, and local lodge minutes
National Union of Mineworkers (South Wales Area) annual reports
Many books on the history and practice of coal mining
Pneumoconiosis research reports

Maritime and Industrial Museum
Maritime Quarter, Swansea
There are on-going exhibitions and a working woollen mill.

Glynn Vivian Art Gallery and Museum

University College of Swansea and Royal Institution of South Wales Museum

PLACES OF INTEREST IN MERTHYR TYDFIL

Merthyr Tydfil Heritage Trust
4 Chapel Road, Merthyr Tydfil
Tel: (01685) 383704

Cyfarthfa Castle Museum and Art Gallery
Cyfarthfa Castle, Brecon Road, Merthyr Tydfil
Tel: (01685) 723112

The Heritage Centre
Ynysfach Road, Merthyr Tydfil
Tel: (01685) 721858

Borough Cemeteries Department
Civic Centre, Castle Street, Merthyr Tydfil
Tel: (01685) 723318
The department holds the Municipal Cemeteries Records from 1860.

Those who are researching Merthyr families may like to know that information on Parish records is held by
Rev. Canon David S. Lee
The Rectory, Thomastown, Merthyr Tydfil.
Tel: (01685) 722992

PLACES OF INTEREST IN BARRY

Living Archive Centre for Barry and The Vale
Memorial Hall, Gladstone Road, Barry
Tel: (01446) 722166

SOUTH EAST WALES

MONMOUTHSHIRE

Monmouth became a shire town in 1536 when the new county was formed and until the local government reorganisation of 1974, with minor boundary adjustments, the area was known as the county of Monmouthshire. It is bounded by Glamorgan in the west along the River Rhymney, in the north and north west by the county of Brecknock, in the north and north east by the county of Herefordshire, in the east by Gloucestershire down to the mouth of the River Wye, then westward along the coast of the Severn estuary and Bristol Channel back to Glamorgan.

The county was divided into six 'hundreds', Abergavenny, Caldicot, Raglan, Skenfrith, Usk and Wentlooge. Newport was the only county borough, the municipal boroughs being Abergavenny and Monmouth. There were 16 urban districts and 5 rural districts with 142 civil parishes.

From prehistoric times the location and the natural resources of the county have attracted immigrants. It became almost a crossroads for the Celts, Saxons, Welsh and in particular the English, transplanting their way of life to where they settled and disturbing the established pattern. Their employment, character, religion and outlook was as varied as the countryside itself.

The county is about 22 miles from east to west and 27 miles from north to south. Only three Welsh counties are smaller in area but its population is easily double that of any other Welsh county except Glamorgan. The north west and west of the county was mainly industrial, providing cargoes for the port of Newport, but from the eastern valley to the River Wye it is rural and agricultural.

The county has produced a number of prominent people. Henry V, who is remembered by a statue in Agincourt Square, was born in Monmouth Castle and it is said that it was the bowmen from his home county who helped him to victory at the Battle of Agincourt. Sir Charles Rolls who, with Royce, gave the world the ultimate in luxury motoring, was born in Monmouth. Lord Nelson is associated with the town and there is a museum in the centre which is dedicated to his life. In recent years excavations in Monmouth have exposed the existence of a busy Medieval town which, together with the Norman arched bridge over the River Monnow, indicates a long-established history. In the more recent past, there was John Frost, Mayor of Newport in 1836, who three years later was arrested for his part in the Chartist uprising and transported to Van Diemen's Land.

The present day population is predominantly English speaking, albeit with a Welsh accent, and the richness of the landscape is matched by the warmth and friendliness of the people. Whether you find your ancestors among the county records or not, you will have the pleasure of searching in what is truly a green and pleasant land.

GWENT RECORD OFFICE

County Hall, Cwmbran, Monmouthshire NP44 2XH
Tel: (01633) 832214

Opening hours

Monday	Closed
Tuesday–Thursday	9.30 a.m.–5.00 p.m.
Friday	9.30 a.m.–4.30 p.m.

On arrival, all visitors should report to the reception desk in the main foyer of County Hall, where they will be directed to the Record Office.

The Record Office is closed on all Bank Holidays and usually for the day following.

Car parking

There is a large Municipal free car park.

Disabled facilities

Disabled visitors can reach the office without negotiating steps.

Appointment system

It is advisable to make an appointment as the office can only accommodate a maximum of ten people at one time.

Reader's ticket

The Office is a member of the County Archives Research Network. Visitors can be issued with tickets on providing some official proof of identification which includes an address, e.g. driving licence, pension book or passport. For those unable to produce satisfactory identification, temporary day tickets are available.

Holdings

Local government records including Quarter Sessions, Monmouthshire and Gwent Councils, borough and district councils

Records dating back to 1250 from individuals and organisations. Parish records of the Church of Wales, and the records of Nonconformist churches; maps, tithe maps, enclosure and older Ordnance Survey maps

Microfiche copies of the 1891 census for the county only. The records held by the office are listed in catalogues and indexes are available for reference in the search room.

(a) General and Topographical index arranged by parish

(b) Personal name index up to 1870

(c) Subject index

A small library of reference books and published works on the history of the county

Postal research

Paid searches of one hour's duration can be undertaken by the staff for those unable to visit the office in person at a cost of £11.75 including VAT. For longer searches, a list of record agents can be supplied.

Facilities

Restaurant, drink vending machines and sandwich shop.

Public telephones

Photocopies can be made subject to the document's physical condition and regulations regarding copyright. A scale of charges is available in the search room

Research information for Monmouthshire will also be found in the Newport Library (see below).

LIBRARIES

Newport Reference Library

Central Library, John Frost Square, Newport, NP9 1PA

Tel: (01633) 211376

Opening Hours

Monday–Wednesday, and Friday 9.30 a.m.–6.00 p.m.
Thursday and Saturday   9.30 a.m.–5.00 p.m.

Car Parking

There is multi-storey parking in the close proximity.

Disabled facilities

A lift is available to the library, which is on the third floor.

Appointment system

It is advisable to make a booking before visiting to ensure the
availability of material, and for microfiche and microfilm readers.

Holdings

Census returns for Monmouthshire 1841–1891
1881 Indexed census for all counties that have been issued
(microfiche).
I.G.I., 1992 edition
St. Catherine's House Indexes (births, deaths and marriages)
1837–1983
Williams Marriage Indexes for Monmouthshire and Glamorgan
Electoral Registers for Newport and Monmouthshire
Trade and Street directories
Monumental Inscriptions, newspapers, maps
A wide selection of books, pamphlets and magazines on genealogy.
Return of Owners of Land 1873 (microfiche except where marked *)
Bedfordshire, Berkshire, Buckinghamshire, Cambridgeshire,
Cornwall, Devon, Dorset, Hertfordshire, Kent, Lancashire,
Lincolnshire, Middlesex*, Northamptonshire, Nottinghamshire,
Somerset, Suffolk, Surrey*, Wales (ex Monmouthshire),
Warwickshire, Wiltshire, Worcestershire, Yorkshire: East Riding,
Yorkshire: West Riding
Also known as 'Modern Domesday,' it lists individuals owning at
least one acre of land. Compiled from Rating Returns.

The staff of the Bibliographical Services at the County library HQ
under the direction of Miss M.L. Gibbens A.L.A. have compiled a book
Bibliography of Gwent. This contains the titles of all the books, papers,
etc. available from the library service. It is available on request in the
Reference section of the Newport Public Library in John Frost Square.

Postal research

Professional research is undertaken by a member of the library staff. Please phone for details and charges.

Facilities

There is no provision for food and drink but the location is amongst shops. Toilets are located outside the research room. The location is only 50 yards from the bus station and about 600 yards from the main line railway station.

Books and publications

Yesterday's Newport, Terry Underwood.

The Way we Were, Terry Underwood.

Through the Century's Eye, Mike Buckingham and Richard Frame.

All are available at the Bookshop within the Library complex.

Pillgwenlly, Newport, Cliff V. Knight, in 4 volumes, Starling Press.

The reference library has a complete list of books about all parts of Gwent which can be seen on request.

REGISTRATION OF BIRTHS, DEATHS AND MARRIAGES

Newport

8 Gold Tops, Newport NP9 4PH
    Marriages   Tel: (01633) 265547
    Births and Deaths Tel: (01633) 262330

Pontypool

Hanbury Road, Pontypool, Torfaen NP4 6NZ
Tel: (01495) 762937

Blackwood

Civic Centre, Pontllanfraith NP2 2YW
Tel: (01495) 226622

Blaenau Gwent RD

'The Grove', Church Street, Tredegar NP2 3DS
Tel: (01495) 722305

Marriages (including copy certificates)

TOURIST OFFICES

Newport
Newport Branch Library Foyer
John Frost Square, Newport NP9 1PA

Blaenau Gwent
Tourism Officer,
Municipal Office, Ebbw Vale, Blaenau Gwent
Tel: (01495) 350555

Torfaen/Pontypool
Tourist Office
Town Hall, Pontypool, Torfaen
Tel: (01495) 762200

Monmouth
Tourist Office
Shire Hall, Agincourt Square, Monmouth. Monmouthshire C.C.
Tel: 01600 713899

Abergavenny
Tourist Information Centre
Swan Meadow, Monmouth Road, Abergavenny, Monmouthshire
Tel: (01873) 857588

Caerleon
Tourist Information Centre
Ffwrrwm Arts and Crafts, High Street, Caerleon, Newport
Tel: (01633) 430777

Chepstow
Tourist Information Centre
Castle Car Park, Bridge Street, Chepstow, Monmouthshire
Tel: (01291) 623772

Cross Keys
Tourist Information Centre
Cwmcarn Forest Drive, Cwmcarn, Caerphilly
Tel: (01495) 272001

Magor
Tourist Information Centre
Granada Services, Junction 23/M4, Magor, Monmouthshire
Tel: (01633) 881122

Wye Valley
Visitors Centre
Jubilee Park, Symonds Yat West
Tel: (01600) 890360

PLACES OF INTEREST IN GWENT

Big Pit Museum
Blaenavon
Tel: (01495) 790311

Chepstow Museum
Gwy House, Bridge Street
Tel: (01291) 625981

Newport Museum and Art Gallery
John Frost Square, Newport
Tel: (01633) 840064

Roman Legionary Museum
High Street, Caerleon
Tel: (01633) 423134

Torfaen Museum Trust
Park Buildings, Park Road, Pontypool
Tel: (01495) 752036

Nelson Museum and Local History Centre
Priory Street, Monmouth NP5 3XA
Tel: (01600) 713519

Tintern Abbey
Tel: (01291) 689251

Tredegar House
Newport
Tel: (01633) 815880

Royal Monmouthshire Royal Engineers (Militia)
Castle and Regimental Museum
The Castle, Monmouth NP5 3BS
Tel: (01600) 712935

Drenewydd Museum
26–27 Lower Row, Butetown, Rhymney
Tel: (01495) 843039

Abergavenny Castle Museum
The Castle, Castle Street
Tel: (01873) 854282

THE NATIONAL LIBRARY OF WALES

Penglais, Aberystwyth, Ceredigion SY23 3BU
Tel: (01970) 623816
Fax: (01970) 615709
JANET: 0000 1300 0006
E-Mail: nlw@aber.ac.uk (to become nlw@llgc.org within the coming year)
Telnet number for the OPAC: 144.124.240.2.
The National Library is situated just outside Aberystwyth on the A487 (Penglais Road).

Opening hours

Monday– Friday   9.30 a.m.– 6.00 p.m.
Saturday (restricted service) 9.30 a.m.– 5.00 p.m.
Sundays and Public Holidays Closed

The Library is closed during the first full week in October for stock taking.

Disabled facilities

Access facilities for the disabled are available at the south (car park) side of the building, and physically handicapped readers are advised to inform the Library of their visits beforehand to ensure maximum assistance.

Reader's ticket

A reader's ticket is needed for research. It is possible to obtain short term (day) tickets by filling in a form at the General Office and providing a document of identification, bearing the applicant's signature. For long term (5 year) tickets, it is necessary to send to the Library for an application form. This also tells the applicant that a reference signature and a passport-type photograph is needed in order to obtain the ticket.

Publications

Since the National Library holds a vast range of resources which are of interest to those researching family history, a very useful leaflet, *Family History at the National Library of Wales: A Concise Guide to Sources*, is available. It not only gives an indication of the records available, but has a concluding section on 'Getting started in family history'. Among the other leaflets which have been produced to help researchers are *Readers' Guide, How to Order Documents, Sources for the History of Houses* and *Maps.*

All these leaflets can be obtained from the National Library together with a list of the many publications which have been produced. These can be bought through booksellers or by sending direct to the above address.

A self-service system is now in operation for microfiche and microfilm in the Microforms Reading Room. This includes the Census Returns, Non-Parochial records, Parish Registers, Calendar of Grants, St. Catherine's House Indexes (OPCS), the I.G.I. and Abstracts of Wills.

Postal research

The Genealogical Research Service into the material in the Library is available for researchers not able to visit. The charge is £14.00 an hour. Information on this service can be obtained from the above address.

Facilities

Meals and refreshments are available Monday to Friday in the basement of the building.

BIBLIOGRAPHY

GENERAL INFORMATION

Welsh Family History, a Guide to Research, John Rowlands et al. (Eds.), The Association of Family History Societies of Wales in conjunction with the Federation of Family History Societies, 1993.

A History of Wales, John Davies, Penguin, 1993.

Parish Registers of Wales, C.J. Williams and J. Watts-Williams, National Library of Wales, 1986.

Non-Conformist Registers of Wales, D. Ifans (Ed.), National Library of Wales, 1994.

Guide to the Department of Manuscripts and Records, National Library of Wales, National Library of Wales, 1994.

Welsh Surnames, T.J. Morgan and Prys Morgan, University of Wales Press, 1985.

A Book of Welsh Names, compiled by Trevor Rendall Davies, Sheppard Press, London, 1952.

A Gazetteer of Welsh Place Names, University of Wales Press, Cardiff, 1989.

An Historic Atlas of Wales, from Early to Modern Times, William Rees, University College Cardiff, Faber and Faber, 1972.

Conquerors and Conquered in Medieval Wales, Ralph Griffiths, Sutton Publishing Ltd.

Royal Commission on Land in Wales and Monmouthshire, (several volumes), 1894. Gives very interesting background information and particular details.

Land and people in Nineteenth Century Wales, David W. Howell, Routledge and Kegan Paul, 1977.

Welsh Convict Women, Deidre Beddoe, Stuart Williams, Barry, 1979. A study of women transported from Wales to Australia 1787–1852.

The Agricultural Community of South-West Wales, David Jenkins, University of Wales Press, 1971.

Patriarchs and Parasites, David W. Howells, University of Wales Press.

Our Mothers Land, Dr. Angela V. John (Ed.), University of Wales Press, 1991.

Lead Mining in Wales, W.J. Lewis, Cardiff University Press, 1967 (with index).

The Welsh Woollen Industry, J. Geraint Jenkins, National Museum of Wales, Cardiff, 1969.

The Surnames of Wales, John and Sheila Rowlands, Federation of Family History Societies, 1996.

NORTH EAST WALES

DENBIGHSHIRE

The Industrial Revolution in North Wales, A.H. Dodd, University of Wales Press, Cardiff, 1951 and reprint.

The Vale of Clwyd: A Short History, D. Winterbottom, 1982.

Llanddulas: Heritage of a Village, B. Jones and M. Rawcliffe, 1985.

The History of Wrexham, A.H. Dodd (Ed.), Hughes and Son, Wrexham, 1957.

Eminent Men of Denbighshire, H. Ellis Hughes, Brython Press, 1946.

The Town of Holt, in County Denbigh, together with the Parish of Isycoed, the Broughtons of Marchwiel, and Notes on the History of Bangor Is y Coed, A.N. Palmer, 1991.

Llansannan: Its History and Associations, T.B. Lowe, 1915.

Ruthin, a Town with a Past, T. Hughes, 1967.

Welsh Genealogies AD 300–1400, P.C. Bartrum, 1974.

Welsh Genealogies AD 1400–1500, P.C. Bartrum, 1983, Studies in Welsh History 4.

The North Wales Quarrymen 1874–1922, Merfyn Jones, University of Wales Press, Cardiff, 1981.

Crwydro Dwyrain Dinbych, F.P. Jones, 1961.

Crwydro Gorllewin Dinbych, F.P. Jones, 1969.

FLINTSHIRE

The History of Flintshire, Vol. 1, C.R. Williams (Ed.), 1961.

They Lived in Flintshire, Vol. 1, H. Williams, 1960.

Northern Flintshire, T.A. Glenn (Ed.), 1913.

History of the Parish of Hawarden, W. Bell Jones, 1943–1945. Unpublished typescript in Clwyd CRO.

Bagillt Through the Ages, Bagillt History Club, 1984.
Buckley and District, T. Cropper, 1923.
The Greenfield Valley: An Introduction to the History and Industrial Archaeology of the Greenfield Valley, K. Davies and C.J. Williams, 1986.
Mold: A Town and its Past, R. Matthias, 1984.
History of Prestatyn, D.W. Davies, 1989.
Maritime History of Rhyl and Rhuddlan, D.W. Davies, 1991.
Guide to the Flintshire Record Office, A.G. Veysey (Ed.), 1974.
The Place Names of East Flintshire, Hywel Wyn Owen, University of Wales Press, Cardiff, 1994. This is the first in a series by the author on the place names of Clwyd.
Crwydro Sir y Fflint, T.I. Ellis, 1959.

NORTH WEST WALES

ISLE OF ANGLESEY/YNYS MON

Anglesey Bibliography, Dewi O. Jones, 1987.
The Day before Yesterday. Anglesey in the 19th Century, E.W. Williams, 1987.
Copper Mountain, John Rowlands, 1981.
Ships and Seamen of Anglesey, Aled Eames, 1973.
Two Centuries of Anglesey Schools, David A. Pretty, 1977.
Portrait of an Island, Helen Ramage, 1987.
Bangor Port of Beaumaris. Shipbuilders and Shipowners, M. Ellis Williams, 1988.
Edwardian Anglesey. A Pictorial History, Vols. 1 and 2, John Cowell, 1991/2.
Anglesey Family Letters, Elizabeth Grace Roberts, 1976.
In Search of Anglesey Ancestry, Elizabeth Grace Roberts, 1973.
The Morris Letters. 18th Century Family Letters, J.H. Davies, 1909.
Mediaeval Anglesey, A.D. Carr, 1982.
Hanes Plwyf Niwbwrch, H. Owen, 1948.
Gwyr Mawr Môn, Bedwyr Lewis Jones, 1979.
Hanes Môn yn y Bedwaredd Ganrif ar Bymtheg, E.A. Williams, 1927.
Cofiant William Morris (1705–1763), Dafydd Wyn Williams, 1995.
Hanes M.C. Môn, Hugh Owen, 1937.

CAERNARFONSHIRE

Old Karnarvon, W.H. Jones, 1984.
A Description of Caernarvonshire (1809–1811), Edmund Hyde Hall.
Portmadoc Ships, Emrys Hughes and Aled Eames, 1975.
The Port Of Caernarfon 1793–1900, Lewis Lloyd, 1989.
The North Wales Quarrymen 1874–1922, E. Merfyn Jones, 1981.
Farming in Caernarvonshire around 1800, R.O. Robert, 1973.
Old Copper Mines of Snowdonia, David Bick, 1963.
The Old Churches of Snowdonia, Hughes and North, 1924.
Transactions of the Caernarvonshire Historical Society, 1939–.
Bangor Port of Beaumaris. Ship Builders and Ship Owners, M. Ellis Williams, 1988.
Fresh as Yesterday. Memories of Old Llanfairfechan, Llanfairfechan Historical Society.
History of the Town of Pwllheli, D. Lloyd Hughes.
Hanes Methodistiaeth Arfon, William Hobley, 1921.
Crwydro Arfon, A. Llewelyn Williams, 1959.
Crwydro Llyn ac Eifionydd, Gruffudd Parry, 1960.
Hynafiaethau Llandegai a Llanllechid, Hugh Derfel, 1979.
Gestiana, Hanes Plwyfi Ynyscynhaearn a Threflys, 1975.
Achau ac Ewyllysiau Teuluoedd de Sir Gaernarfon, T. Ceiri Griffith, 1989.
Hanes Tref Pwllheli, D.G. Lloyd Hughes, 1986.

GWYNEDD

Pedigrees of Anglesey, Caernarfonshire, and Related Families, J.E. Griffith. Includes Merionethshire families.
Bangor Diocese Probate Records Pre 1700, National Library of Wales.
The Diocese of Bangor during Three Centuries, A.I. Price, 1929.
A History of the Quakers in Wales, T.M. Rees, 1925.
Hanes y Wesleyaid Cymreig, Hugh Jones, 1911.
Hanes y Bedyddwr yn Nghymru, J. Spinther James, Carmarthen, 1903.
Bywgraffiadur Cymreig, 1953. Also available in English as *Dictionary of Welsh Biography*.
Rhestr o Enwau Lleoedd, Prifysgol Cymru, 1989.

MERIONETHSHIRE/MEIRIONNYDD

Old Blood of Merioneth. History of the Nanney-Wynn Family, Authir, 1989.

Ship Master. The Life and Letters of Capt. Robert Thomas, Llandanwg, 1843–1903.

The Story of the Parishes of Dolgelly and Llanelltyd, Newtown, 1928.

Walking through Merioneth, G.W. Hall.

Welsh Founders of Pennsylvania, T.A. Glenn, Baltimore, 1970.

The Amity of Aberdyfi, in *National Library of Wales Journal,* XIII(1) (1983), Lewis Lloyd.

The Brig Susannah of Aberdyfi, Lewis Lloyd.

The Unity of Barmouth, Lewis Lloyd, 1977.

Barmouth 1565–1920, Lewis Lloyd, 1993.

The Book of Harlech, Lewis Lloyd, 1987.

Sails on the Mawddach, Lewis Lloyd.

Wherever Freights May Offer. The Maritime Community of Barmouth, Lewis Lloyd 1993.

From Merioneth to Botany Bay, H.J. Owen.

Merioneth Volunteers and Local Militia 1795–1816, H.J. Owen, 1934.

Letters from America, David Jones, 1990.

Merioneth Lay Subsidy Roll 1292–1293, K. Williams-Jones, 1976.

A Calendar of the Merioneth Quarter Sessions 1733–1765, K. Williams-Jones, 1976.

Llanfachreth, Mary Corbett Harries, 1973.

A Short History of the Parish of Llanuwchllyn, William Hughes.

The Story of Aberdyfi, Hugh M. Lewis, 1974.

Atgofion am Llanuwchllyn, E.D. Rowlands, 1975.

Atlas Meirionnydd, Geraint Bowen, 1974.

Noddwyr Beirdd ym Meirion, Glenys Davies, 1974.

Hanes plwyf Llanegryn, William Davies, 1948.

Hanes Bro Trawsfynydd. Merched y Wawr, 1973.

Hanes plwyf Ffestiniog, G.J. Williams.

The staff in the libraries and Record Offices are helpful with the translation of parts of these books when time permits.

CENTRAL WALES

POWYS

Powys, Montgomeryshire Book, Women's Institute and Countryside Books, Newbury, BRK.

Around Llandrindod Wells, Chris Wilson, Chalford Publishing Co., Stroud.

Marching to Zion, J.B. Sinclair and R.W.D. Penn, Cadoc Books, Kington, HEF.

Roots and Branches, T.O. Evans. (This book is out of print but would be available through the Inter-Library Loan Service.)

Kilvert's Diary, William Plomer (Ed.), Penguin.

Epynt Without People . . . and Much More, Ronald Davies, Y Lolfa, Talybont, CMN.

Law and Disorder in Breconshire 1750–1880, Dewi Davies, D.G. and A.F. Evans, Brecon.

SOUTH WEST WALES

CARDIGANSHIRE/CEREDIGION

A Gateway to Wales. A History of Cardigan, W.J. Lewis.

The Ships and Seamen of Southern Ceridigion, Geraint J. Jenkins, Gomer Press, Llandysul, 1982.

Farmers and Figureheads. The Port of New Quay and its Hinterland, S.C. Passmore, Dyfed Cultural Services, 1992.

The Old Metal Mines of Mid-Wales, David E. Bick, Merton Priory Press. A series on non-ferrous metal mining in Cardiganshire, Montgomeryshire and Merionethshire.

Cows, Cardis and Cockneys. Cardiganshire Dairymen in London, Gwyneth Francis-Jones, Welsh Books Centre, 1984

CARMARTHENSHIRE

The Story of Carmarthenshire. Vol. 2 1600s to 1832, A.G. Prys-Jones, C. Davies, Llandybie, 1972.

The Story of Carmarthen, J. and V. Lodwick, St. Peters Press, Carmarthen, revised edition 1994.

Sir Gar. Studies in Carmarthenshire History, Carmarthenshire Antiquarian Society, 1991.

A Shilling for Carmarthen. The Town They Nearly Tamed, Pat Molloy, Gomer, Llandysul, 1981.

Historic Carmarthenshire Homes and their Families, Francis Jones, Carmarthenshire Antiquarian Society, 1987.

Rebecca's Children. A Study of Rural Society, Crime and Protest, David Jones, Clarendon Press, Oxford, 1989.

And They Bless Rebecca. An Account of the Welsh Toll-Gate Riots 1839–1844, Pat Molloy, Gomer, Llandysul, 1983.

Pembrey and Burry Port, their Harbours, Shipwrecks and Looters, Llanelli Borough Council.

PEMBROKESHIRE

Pembrokeshire County History, Vol. 3, 1536–1815; Vol. 4, 1815–1974, David W. Howells (Ed.), Pembrokeshire Historical Society, 1993.
Old Pembrokeshire and Carmarthenshire, Roger N. Davies, Gomer, Llandysul, 1991.
The story of Pembrokeshire, Wendy Hughes, Gwasg Garreg Gwalch, Capel Garmon.
The Landsker Borderlands, Dyfed Archaeological Trust, 1993.
The Tithe War in Pembrokeshire, Pamela Horn, Preseli Printers, Fishguard, 1982.
The Drovers Roads of Wales, Vol. 2, Pembrokeshire and the South. Toulson and Forbes, Whittet Books, London, 1992. Gives a picture of the rural economy.
Burton Parish History, H.J. Dickman, 1984.
Leaflets on individual parishes in South Pembrokeshire, from SPARC, The Old School, Station Road, Narberth. Pembrokeshire.

GLAMORGAN

On The Parish, Raymond K.J. Grant, Glamorgan Record Office, 1988. Based on documentation from Glamorgan.
Glamorgan Hearth Tax Assessments of 1670, Elizabeth Parkinson, South Wales Record Society, 1994.
The South Wales Iron Industry 1750–1885, Laurence Ince, Ferric Publishing.
Glamorgan, its Gentlemen and Yeomanry, 1797–1980, Bryn Owen, Starling Press.
Glamorgan County History, Vol. I, Natural History; Vol. II, Early Glamorgan; Vol. III, The Middle Ages; Vol. IV, Early Modern Glamorgan; Vol. V, Industrial Glamorgan 1700–1970; Vol. VI, Glamorgan Society 1780–1980, Glamorgan History Trust, University of Wales Press. This is an on-going series.
Glamorgan Historian, Vols. 1–12, Stewart Williams, D. Brown and Sons, Cowbridge.
History and Antiquities of Glamorgan 1874, Thomas Nicholas; reprint by Stewart Williams, D. Brown and Sons, Cowbridge, 1970.

Cardiff and the Marquessess of Bute, John Davies, University of Wales Press, 1981. About the estates and land owned by the Marquesses of Bute in Glamorgan 1766–1900.

Glamorgan. Farmhouses and Cottages, Vol. IV, Ecclesiastical Parishes in Glamorgan, HMSO, 1988.

The Story of Ports and Shipping along the Glamorgan Heritage Coast, R.E. Takel, Glamorgan Heritage Coast Joint Management and Advisory Committee, 1982.

A Catalogue of Glamorgan Estate Maps, Hilary M. Thomas, Glamorgan Archives Publication, 1992.

SOUTH EAST WALES

MONMOUTHSHIRE

The History of Monmouthshire from the Coming of the Normans into Wales down to the Present Time, Sir Joseph Bradney. Originally published in 1904. Reprinted in nine volumes by the Merton Priory Press.

The South Wales Iron Industry 1750–1885, Laurence Ince, Merton Priory Press, 1993.

Early Victorian Usk, David R. Lewis, Merton Priory Press, 1988.

For further books on Monmouthshire see the reference to *Bibliography of Gwent* on p. 66.

It is worth noting that books which are not easy to obtain can be requested through the Inter-Library Loan Service, available at most libraries in England and Wales. The current fee for this service is £1.00.

USEFUL ADDRESSES

Capel (The Chapel Heritage Society)
c/o The City and County of Swansea Archives
County Hall, Oystermouth Road
Swansea, County of Swansea SA1 3SN

Companies Registration Office
Companies House, Crown Way
Maindy, Cardiff

Swansea and District Land Registry
Tybryn Glas, High Street
Swansea, County of Swansea

The Public Record Office
Ruskin Avenue, Kew,
Richmond, Surrey TW9 4DU
Tel: (0181) 8763444

The British Library Newspaper Library
Colindale Avenue
London NW9 5HE

Principal Registry of the Family Division
Somerset House
Strand, London WC2R 1LA

Office for National Statistics,
General Register Office
St. Catherine's House, Kingsway
London WC2B 6JP.

Note: This office is due to move during 1997; check for new address.

Federation of Family History Societies (Publications) Ltd.

Administration: The Benson Room
Birmingham and Midland Institute
Margaret Street, Birmingham B3 3BS

Sales: 2–4 Killer Street
Ramsbottom, Bury, Lancs. BL0 9BZ

The Guildhall Library

Aldermanbury
London EC2P 2EJ

National Maritime Museum

Greenwich
London SE10 9NF

British Association for Cemeteries in South Asia

76½ Chartfield Avenue
London SW15 6HQ

Commonwealth War Graves Commission

2 Marlow Road
Maidenhead, Berkshire SL6 7DX

SECRETARIES OF
THE FAMILY HISTORY SOCIETIES OF WALES

Clwyd FHS
>Mrs. M. Andrews
>22 Parc y Llan
>Henllan, Denbighshire LL16 5AS

Dyfed FHS
>Mrs. A. Owen
>Delfan, High Street
>Llandysul, Ceredigion SA44 4DG

Glamorgan FHS
>Mrs. M. Bullows
>The Orchard, Penmark
>Barry, Vale of Glamorgan CF6 9BN

Gwent FHS
>Mr.E.E. Cann
>1a Melbourne Way
>Newport, Newport County Borough NP9 3RE

Gwynedd FHS
>Mrs. J. Hinde
>Cwm Arian, Penysarn Fawr
>Penysarn, Isle of Anglesey LL69 9BX

Powys FHS
>Mrs.V. Brown
>Cwm Kesty Farmhouse
>Newchurch, Kington
>Powys via Hereford HR5 3QR

The Welsh FHSs are based chiefly on the post-1974 Welsh counties: Clwyd (covering the pre-1974 counties of Denbigh, Flint and part of Merioneth), Dyfed (Cardigan, Carmarthen and Pembroke), Glamorgan (Glamorgan), Gwent (Monmouthshire), Gwynedd (Anglesey, Caernarfon and Merioneth), and Powys (Brecon, Montgomery and Radnor).

WALES IN 1996

Local Authority Changes

Even as we prepare the information in this booklet we are aware of the plans for changes in Local Government in Wales in 1996. The Unitary Authorities which are planned will bring new names to some of the regions of Wales. However, we feel that most of the records which you need for your research are likely to remain where they are for some time to come and we have decided to proceed with the information that we have, while listing the new Authorities with the addresses of the administrative centres.

NORTH EAST WALES

Denbighshire County Council
 c/o Council Offices
 Wynnstay Road, Ruthin LL15 1YN
 Tel: (01824) 702201

Flintshire County Council
 Shire Hall
 Mold CH7 6NB
 Tel: (01352) 704476

Conwy County Borough Council
 Bodlondeb
 Conwy LL32 8DU
 Tel: (01492) 574000

Wrexham County Borough Council
 Guildhall
 Wrexham LL11 1AY
 Tel: (01987) 292107

NORTH WEST WALES

Cyngor Sir Ynys Môn/Isle of Anglesey County Council
Swyddfa'r Sir
Llangefni, Isle of Anglesey LL77 7TW
Tel: (01248) 750057

Gwynedd County Council
Swyddfa'r Sir, County Offices
Caernarfon LL55 1SH
Tel: (01286) 672255

CENTRAL WALES

Powys County Council
County Hall
Llandrindod Wells, Powys LD1 5LG
Tel: (01597) 826000

SOUTH WEST WALES

Ceredigion County Council
Penmorfa
Aberaeron, Ceredigion SA46 0PA
Tel: (01545) 570881

Carmarthenshire County Council
County Hall
Carmarthen SA31 1LE
Tel: (01267) 234567

Pembrokeshire County Council
Cambria House
Haverfordwest, Pembrokeshire SA61 2DN
Tel: (01437) 764551

GLAMORGAN AND THE COUNTY OF SWANSEA

Neath and Port Talbot County Borough Council
Civic Centre
Port Talbot SA13 1PJ
Tel: (01639) 875200

Bridgend County Borough Council
PO Box 4, Civic Offices
Angel Street, Bridgend CF31 1LX
Tel: (01656) 643643

Vale of Glamorgan County Borough Council
Civic Offices, Holton Road
Barry CF63 4RU
Tel: (01446) 700111

Rhondda, Cynon, Taff County Borough Council
Clydach Vale
Tel: (01443) 424000

County Borough Council of Merthyr Tydfil
Civic Centre
Merthyr Tydfil CF47 8AN
Tel: (01685) 723201

Caerphilly County Borough Council
Ystrad Fawr
Ystrad Mynach, Hengoed CF8 7SF
Tel: (01443) 815588

Cardiff County Council
County Hall
Atlantic Wharf, Cardiff CF1 5UW
Tel: (01222) 872000

The County of Swansea
County Hall
The County of Swansea SA1 3SN
Tel: (01792) 471111

SOUTH EAST WALES

Blaenau Gwent County Borough Council
Municipal Offices
Civic Centre, Ebbw Vale NP3 6XN
Tel: (01495) 350555

Torfaen County Borough Council
Civic Centre
Pontypool NP4 6YB
Tel: (01495) 762200

Monmouthshire County Council
c/o County Hall
Cwmbran, Monmouthshire NP44 2XH
Tel: (01633) 838838
Newport County Borough Council
Civic Centre
Newport, South Wales NP9 4UR
Tel (01633) 244491

These areas of South Wales would appear to be facing the greatest changes but when the new authorities settle down it is likely that the records you need will still be in the Record Offices and Libraries of the towns which are listed in this book.